The Myth Awakens

THE MYTH AWAKENS

Canon, Conservatism, and Fan Reception
of **STAR WARS**

EDITED BY
Ken Derry
AND
John C. Lyden

CASCADE *Books* • Eugene, Oregon

THE MYTH AWAKENS
Canon, Conservatism, and Fan Reception of *Star Wars*

Cascade Books
An Imprint of Wipf and Stock Publishers
199 W. 8th Ave., Suite 3
Eugene, OR 97401

www.wipfandstock.com

PAPERBACK ISBN: 978-1-5326-1973-1
HARDCOVER ISBN: 978-1-4982-4627-9
EBOOK ISBN: 978-1-4982-4626-2

Cataloguing-in-Publication data:

Names: Derry, Ken, editor. | Lyden, John C., editor.

Title: The myth awakens : canon, conservatism, and fan reception of *Star Wars* / Edited by Ken Derry and John C. Lyden.

Description: Eugene, OR: Cascade Books, 2018 | Includes bibliographical references and index.

Identifiers: ISBN 978-1-5326-1973-1 (paperback) | ISBN 978-1-4982-4627-9 (hardcover) | ISBN 978-1-4982-4626-2 (ebook)

Subjects: LCSH: Star Wars films—Religious aspects.

Classification: PN1995.9 M696 2018 (print) | PN1995.9 (ebook)

Thanks to the following for permission to use their creative work: Kutter Callaway, Denis Achilles del Callar, Lisa Gerlsbeck, Santiago Gomez, Mike J. Nichols, and Christian Waggoner.

Manufactured in the U.S.A.   09/12/18

To *Star Wars* fans everywhere, especially my three children, Karl, Grace, and Clara.

J. C. L.

To my family: my parents, Bob and Carol, who showed me how to be joyful; Mark, Yordest, and Ella, who keep me smiling; Agnes, Ron, and Tracy, for their support and their silliness; and Kelly, who is everything.

K. D.

"Kid, I've flown from one side of this galaxy to the other, and I've seen a lot of strange stuff, but I've never seen *anything* to make me believe that there's one all-powerful Force controlling everything."—Han Solo

CONTENTS

ACKNOWLEDGMENTS

John would like to thank Ken for twisting his arm to do this project, and for being a scrupulous and punctilious editor with an eye for both detail and concept. Ken in turn wishes to thank John for letting his arm be twisted, and for his grace and wisdom in all things related to both editing and *Star Wars*.

Together we would like to express our tremendous gratitude to the contributors to this volume for their great humor, collegiality, and scholarship; they have been a wonderful group to work with and we very much look forward to celebrating with them in person the next time we meet. Among this group we wish to particularly highlight the personal and intellectual fabulousness of Kutter Callaway, since it was his idea that we make *The Myth Awakens* in the first place. As the book's origins lie in a session at the American Academy of Religion, we would be remiss if we did not mention the great work of Robert Puckett, the Director of the annual AAR meeting. Robert has consistently been an impassioned supporter of genuine academic community and of scholarly work that pushes boundaries, work that at times may flout convention by being just a little bit fun (in all the right ways). For their immense practical help with the day-to-day critical details required to complete a project like this, we are very grateful to the outstanding team at Wipf and Stock who worked so patiently with us: Rodney Clapp, Calvin Jaffarian, Brian Palmer, and Matthew Wimer. And of course this book would not have been possible at all without the fans and creators of *Star Wars*, who are a true Force in this universe.

Finally, we wish to thank our families so very, very much, for all of their encouragement, patience, and love.

CONTRIBUTORS

Joseph Boston is a social worker, currently residing in Brisbane, Australia. He is an Afro-pessimist and autodidact, dread in Babylon, Baldwin to a trap beat. He has seen God and her name is Octavia Butler.

Joshua Call is Professor of English at Grand View University in Des Moines, Iowa. His publications include co-editing *Dungeons, Dragons, and Digital Denizens: The Digital Role-Playing Game* (2012), and *Guns, Grenades, and Grunts: First-Person Shooter Games* (2012). Josh earned his most recent lightsaber as a reward for finishing academic writing projects, and is still hoping for an acceptance letter into the Jedi Academy.

Kutter Callaway is Assistant Professor of Theology and Culture, Fuller Theological Seminary, Pasadena, California. His publications include *Scoring Transcendence* (2012), *Watching TV Religiously* (2016), and *Breaking The Marriage Idol* (2018). A lifelong *Star Wars* fan, he is currently engaged in a harebrained craft project with his daughters involving the re-creation of the entire Imperial fleet out of collected wine corks.

Ken Derry is Associate Professor of Religion, Teaching Stream, in the Department of Historical Studies at the University of Toronto. His published essays have considered the relationship between religion and violence in a range of written and visual creative works, including John Woo's *The Killer*, contemporary Indigenous literature, *The Wizard of Oz*, and the Netflix series *Luke Cage*. Ken has also written about pedagogy and the study of religion, and will neither confirm nor deny that he has used Taylor Swift's "Shake it Off" to explain Michel Foucault's views on authorship and ideology.

Daniel White Hodge is Associate Professor of Intercultural Communication at North Park University, Chicago. His publications include *Heaven Has A Ghetto* (2009), *The Soul Of Hip Hop* (2010), and *Hip Hop's Hostile Gospel* (2017). Yet, what remains his most cherished accomplishment is his award-winning brisket and baby back ribs. Daniel also has a working AT-AT he has leashed in his office.

Syed Adnan Hussain is Assistant Professor of Religious Studies at Saint Mary's University, Halifax. His research and publications are primarily in modern Islam as well as religion and popular culture. He worked in game stores all through his teens and plans to someday turn his employee perk collectibles into a new kitchen. But presently he really wishes he had known about Daniel White Hodge's brisket when the AAR was in Chicago.

Chris Klassen teaches in the Religion and Culture department at Wilfrid Laurier University, Waterloo. Her publications include *Religion and Popular Culture: A Cultural Studies Approach* (Oxford University Press, 2014). She also knits. All the time. Even in class, sometimes. She has not yet managed the life-sized R2-D2 pattern, though. Nor the golden bikini.

John C. Lyden is Liberal Arts Core Director and Professor of Liberal Arts at Grand View University, Des Moines. He is the author of *Film as Religion: Myths, Morals, and Rituals* (2003), editor of the *Routledge Companion to Religion and Film* (2009), and co-editor (with Eric Michael Mazur) of the *Routledge Companion to Religion and Popular Culture* (2015). John has also been editor of the *Journal of Religion & Film* since 2011. He saw the original *Star Wars* film so many times when it first came out that he memorized most of the dialogue, and can still plausibly impersonate most of the voices.

Kenneth MacKendrick completed his doctoral dissertation on the early writings of Jürgen Habermas at the Centre for the Study of Religion, University of Toronto. He is working on *Evil: A Critical Primer* for Equinox Press and has recently written essays on myth-making and superheroes, imaginary companions, and the writings of Chuck Palahniuk. Ken has been teaching Defence Against the Dark Arts in the Department of Religion, University of Manitoba since 2002 and is a volunteer member of the Carol Corps.

Lindsay Macumber is an Adjunct Professor at Saint Mary's and Dalhousie University, Halifax, where she specializes in Religion and Popular Culture, Judaism, and Twentieth-Century European history. Her doctoral dissertation at the University of Toronto focused on Hannah Arendt's representation of the Holocaust. In her "spare" time she trains her two-year-old youngling in the ways of the Force.

Justin Mullis has an MA in Religious Studies from the University of North Carolina at Charlotte where he has also lectured on *Jurassic Park, King Kong,* and *The Planet of the Apes.* His work primarily deals with the intersection of religion and popular-culture, and includes explorations of H.P. Lovecraft's Cthulhu Mythos in *The Journal of the Fantastic in the Arts* 26.3 and adult male fans of *My Little Pony: Friendship is Magic* in *The Retro-Futurism of Cuteness* (Punctum Books). While Justin appreciates *Star Wars'* many ardent fans his own loyalty is to Japanese *kaijū* movies, which he has written about for the book *Giant Creatures in Our World* (McFarland).

Photo courtesy of Kutter Callaway.

ILLUSTRATIONS

PREFACE

The Book Awakens

KEN DERRY

This project began not so long ago and not so far away, as a collection of academic presentations at the November 2016 annual meeting of the American Academy of Religion (AAR), which took place in San Antonio, Texas. The session was offered by one of the AAR's many program units, the Religion, Film, and Visual Culture group, of which I am co-chair (and John Lyden is former co-chair). The idea for the session had been proposed the year before, in the wake of angry fan responses to trailers for *Star Wars Episode VII: The Force Awakens*. These early glimpses indicated that the film would feature two central characters, Rey and Finn, who are not white men. As Josh, Dan, and Joseph[1] discuss in their chapters in this book, a good amount of the anger directed at the trailers came from white supremacists, who claimed that such a shift in *Star Wars* away from the blond, blue-eyed, male protagonists of yore was an example of "white genocide."

Responses to *The Force Awakens* when it appeared in theatres in December, 2015, continued to focus on its relationship to key aspects of the earlier installments in the franchise—plot, characters, moral vision,

1. Note that in this Preface and in my Introduction I deliberately refer to the contributors to this book by their first names (with their permission). I knew some of them before we started working on this project together, and I definitely know all of them now, at least to some extent. Referring to other scholars by their surnames is an academic convention that can serve a useful purpose on some occasions; often, however, it strikes me as an unnecessary formality that obscures our actual relationships with one another. Academic fields are notoriously small, and often many if not all of the people working in a given area of study will know one another well. Certainly in person and over email we call each other by our first names; why not also do it in print?

etc. The film was immediately both censured and praised for the degree to which it reiterated elements of the original trilogy; while some critics and fans expressed concerns over this cinematic recycling, many who hated the prequel trilogy returned to the fold satisfied. In a sense, it seemed that the "myth" that was so much a part of the first three films had been absent or "asleep" during the prequels, and had been awakened by the newest addition to the universe created by George Lucas 40 years earlier. In considering these reactions, the AAR session in 2016 examined the new film in relation to *Star Wars* fandom and notions of "myth." The session consisted of three separate talks, plus a response, and resulted in some exceptionally thoughtful conversations among those who attended about myth, *Star Wars*, fandom, and the academic study of religion itself. Inspired by these conversations, the event's presider, Kutter Callaway—a long-time *Star Wars* fan himself—suggested that we think about turning the session into a book. After finding several other scholars whose work intersected with considerations of religion and *Star Wars* in some respect, and who had the time and interest to take part in this project, we were on our way.

The authors we assembled for this book investigate in various ways the religious ramifications of the mythic awakening initiated by the release of Episode VII. Drawing on a wide variety of theoretical tools, they reflect on how a cultural mythology has been renewed and received by fans. Much of this reception has in fact been very positive, with the most vocal (and often objectionable) objections—like those of the aforementioned white supremacists—arising precisely from the ways in which *The Force Awakens* deviates from the template laid down long, long ago, in a galaxy far, far away. Both the affirming and critical responses to the film, however, suggest that there is a deeply conservative aspect to myth, that in part at least its power lies in its ability to reinforce "traditional" values. Thus, while appearing socially progressive in some ways, for example, *The Force Awakens* may arguably be re-inscribing certain stereotypes of race and gender, as well as notions of American exceptionalism and political dualism that have become increasingly problematic in the decades since the original film.

Not surprisingly, this pattern of conservative responses to *The Force Awakens* was repeated after the opening of the film's sequel, *Episode VIII: The Last Jedi*. Many fans, for example, were clearly angered by the movie's deviations from the traditional *Star Wars* myth. The most visible example of such a response was the online petition to remove *The Last Jedi* from the *Star Wars* canon, because it "completely destroyed the legacy of Luke

Skywalker and the Jedi."[2] More egregiously, some fans were upset—as they were with *The Force Awakens*—at the prominent role of women in the film.[3] Kelly Marie Tran, the first woman of color to play a lead role in the entire *Star Wars* franchise, received online sexist and racist harassment for her role as Rose Tico.[4] Although there were certainly some positive reactions to the film, the overall fan assessment of Episode VIII is extremely low: on the aggregate site *Rotten Tomatoes*, for example, the audience score for the film is just 46 percent. In contrast, The *Force Awakens'* score is 88 percent.[5] This disparity may well be connected to the fact that *The Last Jedi* strays much, much farther from the *Star Wars* path than *Force* does, and so fans in general like it much, much less.[6]

2. Walsh, "Have Disney"; see also Sharf, "Petition to Remove."

3. One such fan even created a version of the movie titled *The Last Jedi: De-Feminized Fanedit* (aka *The Chauvinist Cut*). This version literally *removes* most of the women from the story, and makes several other changes to ensure that none of the male characters (or, presumably, viewers) have to feel emasculated. Thus, as described on *Pirate Bay* where the torrent file was uploaded, in this version of the film: "Leia never scolds, questions nor demotes Poe"; "Kylo is more badass and much less conflicted and volatile"; there is "no superpowered Rey"; and the character of Holdo has been deleted, which not only means we don't see her "scold" Poe either, but that in fact, heroically, "the Kamikaze is carried out by Poe." With all these gendered alterations, we're told, the film "can now at least be viewed without feeling nauseaus (sic)." For an account of this fan-edit, including responses to it from the director and stars of *The Last Jedi*, see Amatulli, "Someone Edited"; for a discussion of complaints about the film that are rooted in sexism see Hillman, "Why so many men."

4. On the other hand, thankfully, many responded to this abuse by affirming the value of Tico's character and condemning the hatred directed at Tran. Pauline Reyes offers an account of both negative and positive responses to Tran/Tico ("The Last Jedi").

5. These are the scores as of February 23, 2018.

6. The low audience score for *The Last Jedi* may relate to an issue that Justin discusses in his essay in this book, namely the possibility that myth and art are inherently oppositional. Myth in this understanding requires stability and consistency, while art is only possible if one is willing to push against boundaries and enact meaningful change. A good myth will be popular but safe, while good art will often be challenging or even upsetting. Perhaps not coincidentally, then, *Jedi* not only has the lowest audience rating on *Rotten Tomatoes* of any live-action *Star Wars* film, but also the greatest gap between popular and professional assessments: the "Top Critics" score for the film is currently 96 percent, which is exactly *twice* the audience score. In addition, several of these critics specifically use terms like "art" and "artful" to describe the film. Norm Wilner, for example, asserts that *The Last Jedi* is "an art-house work" that "takes our heroes into strange, unexpected territory" and "breathes in a way that *The Force Awakens* didn't, developing these new characters while also considering the larger themes of the franchise for what feels like the first time" ("Star Wars").

While there is much that could be said about responses to *The Last Jedi*, we say very little of it in this book. As of this writing (in February, 2018), the film has only been out for two months; it is still quite early to be able to properly examine fan reactions to it. Also, the ten essays in this book were all written in the first half of 2017, more than six months before Episode VIII appeared in theaters. As a result these essays examine notions of myth and conservatism as they relate to fandom and *Star Wars*, with particular attention paid to *The Force Awakens* and virtually none paid to *The Last Jedi*.[7] Very briefly and broadly, the lenses that each author uses for this task include:

- Me: academia and play
- John: allegory and politics
- Lindsay: allegory and psychology
- Chris: psychology and gender
- Kutter: music and gender
- Dan and Joseph: "race" and gender
- Josh: "race" and canon
- Justin: canon and fandom
- Adnan: canon and memory
- Ken: canon and authority

Beyond a general focus on myth and conservatism we did not ask authors to address any particular issues or questions, but a number of patterns emerged. Given the great importance of Joseph Campbell's work on myth to Lucas's films, many of the essays not surprisingly make at least passing mention of this work, with John, Lindsay, and Chris all spending some time thinking about Campbell's ideas in new ways in relation to *Star Wars*. Most of the chapters also address questions of power and marginalization, of how *Star Wars* and its reception create certain boundaries, classifications, and hierarchies, thereby suggesting who and what does and does not "count," and in what ways. The chapters by Chris, Kutter, Dan, Joseph, and Josh tackle these questions directly by focusing on issues of gender and race. Virtually everyone also considers the notion of "canon" and this franchise

7. Because editing on this book could not begin until early 2018 a few authors were able to add some remarks about *The Last Jedi* to their discussions. All of us agreed, however, that the film does not impact our analyses of religion and fandom and *Star Wars* in any significant ways.

in some respect, with three contributors—Justin, Adnan, and Ken—explicitly using this notion as a way to interrogate the category of "religion."

My own introduction to this book picks up on another common thread that runs through everyone's contributions, which is a self-reflexive consideration of our roles as scholars. That is to say, the essays that follow use *Star Wars* to address, explicitly or implicitly, questions about the academic study of religion itself—what it is, what it could be, what it should be. As with the *Star Wars* universe, this field of study is affected in critical ways by members of a community. Even Lucas himself never had the final say about his own creations, but has always been in (often tense) conversation with fans. Which is to say that, in these contexts, Han Solo was right: there is no single all-powerful transcendent Force controlling everything, whether in *Star Wars* or in the study of religion. There are, rather, various human forces that shape the academic and pop culture universes in which we live and find meaning—and we all participate in this shaping.

Ken Derry, February 2018
Toronto

Bibliography

Amatulli, Jenna. "Someone Edited 'The Last Jedi' To Make A 'Chauvinist Cut' Without Women." *Huffington Post.* January 1, 2018. http://www.huffingtonpost.ca/entry/edited-the-last-jedi-chauvinist-women_us_5a5e1d6ee4b04f3c55a63b27.

Hillman, Melissa. "Why so many men hate *The Last Jedi* but can't agree on why." *Bitter Gertrude.* January 4, 2018. https://bittergertrude.com/2018/01/04/why-so-many-men-hate-the-last-jedi-but-cant-agree-on-why.

Reyes, Pauline. "'The Last Jedi' star Kelly Marie Tran defended by fans from racist, sexist comments." *InqPOP.* December 28, 2017. http://pop.inquirer.net/2017/12/the-last-jedi-star-kelly-marie-tran-defended-by-fans-from-racist-sexist-comments.

Sharf, Zack. "Petition to Remove 'Star Wars: The Last Jedi' From Official Canon Has Over 13,000 Signatures." *IndieWire.* December 19, 2017. http://www.indiewire.com/2017/12/petition-star-wars-last-jedi-remove-canon-signatures-1201909099.

Walsh, Henry. "Have Disney strike Star Wars Episode VIII from the official canon." *change.org.* Accessed February 24, 2018. https://www.change.org/p/the-walt-disney-company-have-disney-strike-star-wars-episode-viii-from-the-official-canon.

Wilner, Norm. "Star Wars: The Last Jedi is the first film in the franchise made by an artist, not a craftsman." *NOW Communications.* December 12, 2017. https://nowtoronto.com/movies/reviews/star-wars-the-last-jedi-review.

INTRODUCTION

Being Sith Lord Sexypants

KEN DERRY

Abstract: Amazingly, this is the first book on *Star Wars* written from the perspective of the academic study of religion. There are many possible reasons why no previous books on this topic have been produced by religion scholars; one of them is very likely that popular culture generally, and *Star Wars* in particular, is not taken seriously enough by many in this field. This situation needs to change for many reasons. Among these is the possibility that examining data that is not considered to be earth-shatteringly important may encourage academics who specialize in religion to be more objective, attentive, and flexible when developing both specific interpretations and broad theories. In short, studying *Star Wars* may in fact help us be better scholars.

"I would only believe in a god who knew how to dance. And when I saw my devil I found him serious, thorough, profound, solemn: he was the spirit of gravity—through him all things fall."
—Friedrich Nietzsche, *Thus Spake Zarathustra*[1]

IN 2015, when many people were eagerly anticipating the first *Star Wars* film in over thirty years to feature the principal members of the original cast, another (smaller, but for many of us just as important)

---

1. My thanks to Michael Kaler—scholar, musician, and bon vivant—for bringing this quote to my attention during a chat at his favorite table at Future Bakery in The Annex, Toronto.

cultural phenomenon from the 1980s re-appeared: the fabled comic strip *Bloom County*, by Berkeley Breathed. Like the *Star Wars* films, *Bloom County* had long ago veered quite far from its origins—becoming *Outland* in 1989, a strip with almost entirely new characters set in a completely different universe—only to disappear entirely in 1995.[2] And like *Star Wars: The Force Awakens*, when *Bloom County* returned it looked very much like the original, but with a few important differences. This was not the world of the first Apple computers and actual newspapers and President Reagan. This was a world of iPhones and the Internet and President Trump.[3] The new comics mixed the comforting familiarity of the past with exciting, sometimes terrifying, jolts of contemporary culture. It was a great blending of the old and the new. And sometimes, as it happened, it was about *Star Wars*.[4]

One of these times involved a new character, "Sam the Lion," a young boy with leukemia who is very much a *Star Wars* fan. On December 2 and 3, 2015, the daily *Bloom County* strips showed Steve Dallas, Republican and defense attorney, being kidnapped by two children, Milo and Binkley, and *Bloom County*'s most popular character, the penguin Opus.[5] Steve is taken to Sam's hospital room, where he is to play—willingly or not—the role of villain to Sam's Jedi hero. Blindfolded and confused Steve is initially very resistant to whatever is going on. In the following Sunday's December 6 full-color strip, he is set free and confronts his abductors. And while Steve bravely tries to maintain his normally selfish stance, his right to do whatever he wants whenever he wants, he is quickly won over by Sam's vulnerability and large pleading eyes. Steve dons a blanket and a bedpan and proclaims himself "Sith Lord Sexypants," to Sam (and everyone's) great delight.[6]

---

2. The strip was resurrected in 2003 for a short while, with a Sunday-only comic called *Opus*.

3. As it happens, *Bloom County* in the 1980s offered several amazingly barbed satiric swipes at Donald Trump—but the fact that he was decidedly *not* the President of the United States marks that time as very different than our own in some crucial ways.

4. In fact there were so many *Star Wars* references in the new strips that when they were collected into a printed book, it was titled *Bloom County Episode XI: A New Hope*. The back cover featured a poster that referenced elements of *The Force Awakens* and was titled "Dork Wars: Adulthood Takes a Nap."

5. These strips are available at http://www.gocomics.com/bloom-county/2015/12/2 and http://www.gocomics.com/bloom-county/2015/12/3.

6. See http://www.gocomics.com/bloom-county/2015/12/6.

There is a lot going on in the December 6 comic that I really like, and that, in terms of how *Star Wars* fandom is represented, relates directly to the study of religion. We could wonder about the varied and varying motives of the different characters to take part in the role-playing; about what it means to "believe" (or not) in what they are doing; about ritual and spontaneity; about how the relationship of the characters to *Star Wars* impacts their relationships with one another. For now I would like to highlight two main issues, which in their own ways relate back to all of the others:

- Taking things seriously: A key point in the comic is that *Star Wars*—and perhaps by extension popular culture in general—*matters*. It is very, very important to some people. It can even matter to people (like Steve Dallas) who do not care at all about *Star Wars*.

- Taking things not so seriously: Part of how *Star Wars* matters to these characters is in the way they play with it. A young boy invents "Sam the Lion" as a way of coping with his illness, while Steve Dallas joins the helpful game by becoming "Sith Lord Sexypants."

In this introduction I want to think a little about the ways in which *Star Wars* and fandom, along with scholars of religion, do and do not (or, sometimes, should and should not) take themselves and their interests seriously.

Star Wars and the Study of Religion

Shockingly, this book you are reading is the first one on *Star Wars* written from the perspective of the academic study of religion.[7] To be completely candid, this statement absolutely *amazes* me. I have read several essays on *Star Wars* over the years by religion scholars, and had always just assumed

---

7. Specifically, nine of the eleven contributors to this book did their graduate training in religion departments, teach/have taught in such departments, and/or are regular participants in academic religion conferences. Interestingly, a quick search reveals that there are at least two books on Star Trek by religion scholars: *Star Trek and Sacred Ground* (1999), edited by Jennifer Porter and Darcee McLaren; and *Religions of Star Trek* (2001), edited by Ross Kraemer, William Cassidy, and Susan Schwartz. There are also studies by religion scholars of science fiction more broadly, such as Douglas Cowan's *Sacred Space* (2010) and Steven Hrotic's *Religion in Science Fiction* (2014). As much as I find the absence of similar work on *Star Wars* discouraging, the existence of these other books gives me hope for the future of the academic study of religion as a field that will not restrict itself to looking at data that, as discussed below, reinforces disciplinary biases such as those regarding texts, gender, and history.

that there were entire books by such authors on this topic out there, some-where. In doing research for this project, however, every time I found a likely candidate it turned to vapor as soon as I looked at it too closely, like Darth Vader striking down Obi-Wan. One such book is John C. McDowell's *The Gospel According to Star Wars* (2007). McDowell has been a professor of theology and religious studies in both the U.K. and Australia. But while his book is insightful and very well researched it is not an academic study of religion and *Star Wars*; it is instead a work of theology. That is to say, as McDowell explains in his introduction, his book is a consideration of the ways in which God may (or may not) be speaking to us through Lucas' films.[8] I encountered a different problem when examining Matthew Ka-pell and John Shelton Lawrence's edited collection, *Finding the Force of the Star Wars Franchise* (2006). Although neither editor is a scholar of religion per se, Lawrence in particular has contributed tremendously to the study of religion and American popular culture. And although their book, like McDowell's, is excellent in many ways, it includes only two chapters out of seventeen that are on the topic of religion, written by scholars of religion (Jennifer Porter and Rachel Wagner).

In stark contrast to this situation there is an *enormous* number of popular/non-academic books dealing in some way with *Star Wars* and religion,[9] as well as books on this topic by scholars in fields such as cinema studies, English literature, and philosophy.[10] As with Kapell and Lawrence's text, some of the examples from this latter group do include a few chapters by religion scholars, but in every case these comprise a small portion of the work as a whole. The following list represents a tiny fraction of all the avail-able books, both popular and academic, on *Star Wars* and religion:

- Frank Allnut, *The Force of Star Wars: Unlocking the Mystery of the Force* (1977)

- Matthew Bortolin, *The Dharma of Star Wars* (2005)

- Douglas Brode and Leah Deyneka (editors), *Sex, Politics, and Religion in Star Wars: An Anthology* (2012)

8. McDowell, *The Gospel*, xix–xxii.

9. Many of these books are, like McDowell's, themselves religious. For a discussion of such texts on religion and *Star Wars*, particularly the Christian ones, see Cowan, *Sacred Space*, 264–9.

10. There will also soon be a full issue of the *Journal of Religion and Popular Culture* devoted to *Star Wars*; the deadline for submissions was March 31, 2017.

- Steven A. Galipeau, *The Journey of Luke Skywalker: An Analysis of Modern Myth and Symbol* (2001)

- Caleb Grimes, *Star Wars Jesus: A Spiritual Commentary on the Reality of the Force* (2006)

- Michael J. Hanson and Max S. Kay, *Star Wars: The New Myth* (2002)

- Mary Henderson: *Star Wars: The Magic of Myth* (1997)

- Steven Rosen, *The Jedi in the Lotus:* Star Wars *and the Hindu Tradition* (2011)

- Kevin J. Wetmore, *The Empire Triumphant: Race, Religion and Rebellion in the Star Wars Films* (2005)

This list raises an obvious question: given how incredibly popular the topic of *Star Wars* and religion is, why has so little work on it been done by *scholars* of religion? Most likely, as John Lyden and others have discussed, it is because there remains a bias in this field against studies of popular culture more broadly, a belief that *Star Wars* movies, for example, or fans' responses to those movies, should not be taken seriously as "real" religion.[11] John himself has been a key voice arguing against this perspective, making it clear why studies of *Star Wars* should absolutely be done by academics specifically trained to study religion.[12]

One of John's key points in this argument involves the critical fact that, while religion scholars might not think much of *Star Wars*, its fans *do* take it very seriously indeed; in fundamental ways it *matters* to them. As he points out, "the narratives in question have potentially contributed

---

11. Lyden, "Whose Film." Other scholars who John points to as pushing back against the idea that popular culture does not constitute worthwhile data for the study of religion include David Chidester, Eric Mazur, and Kate McCarthy (ibid., 782–3). In addition, Mary Ann Beavis, Scott Daniel Dunbar, and Chris Klassen recently put forth an extended argument on this topic—in the context of discussing the academic purposes served by the *Journal of Religion and Popular Culture* (*JRPC*)—that echoes and expands on the points that John makes regarding religion and *Star Wars*. As they summarize in the article's abstract: "The *JRPC* produces scholarship on the myriad ways in which religion is presented, produced, studied, interpreted, rationalised, manufactured and disseminated in popular culture. . . . Popular culture is an indicator of the type of activities that have gained prominence in mass media for conveying religious meaning, purpose and communal experience. The ubiquity of religious themes and experiences in popular culture necessitates their continued academic study" (Beavis et al., "The *Journal*," 421).

12. See, e.g., Lyden, "Whose Film" and "Apocalyptic Determinism." Others who have made the case for seeing *Star Wars* as worthy of study by religion scholars include Bowen and Wagner, "Hokey Religions"; Daley-Bailey, "Star Wars"; and Porter, "I Am a Jedi."

in some significant way to the formation of communal identity, a set of shared ideas about ultimate meaning and values, and a set of practices that reinforce or express these."[13] And, famously, Lucas from the start seems to have intended to have exactly this kind of impact. Reflecting on his creation of the franchise in an interview from the late 1990s, he declared: "Somebody has to tell young people what we think is a good person. I mean, we should be doing it all the time. That's what the Iliad and the Odyssey are about—'This is what a good person is; this is who we aspire to be.' You need that in a society. It's the basic job of mythology."[14] One of the notoriously tricky things about myths, though, is that they are not always exactly clear about what they are trying to tell us—and this is as true of *Star Wars* as it is of any traditional sacred text.[15] Lucas undoubtedly succeeded in crafting a story that people care about deeply, that has a real and measurable impact on their lives.[16] But the ways in which they care,

13. Lyden, "Whose Film," 782.

14. Rayment, "Master of the Universe," 20. In another interview from the late 1990s, Lucas similarly stated: "I wanted [*Star Wars*] to be a traditional moral study, to have some sort of palpable precepts in it that children could understand. There is always a lesson to be learned. Where do these lessons come from? Traditionally, we get them from church, the family, art, and in the modern world we get them from the media—from movies" (Seabrook, "Why is the Force").

15. For a detailed examination of the inherent, mythic ambiguity in *Star Wars* (from the perspective of literary and cultural studies) see Flotmann, *Ambiguity*.

16. Not everyone agrees that this impact makes the culture of *Star Wars* similar to traditional religions in any meaningful way, however. Religion scholar Wendy Doniger, for one, laments the "degraded mythology" that people might find "in films and children's books" (*Other People's Myths*, 131–2; cited in Lyden, "Whose Film," 781). Neo-atheist Sam Harris, on the other hand, applauds such "degraded mythology" precisely for being a shadow of its "real" religious counterparts: "Imagine a world in which generations of human beings come to believe that certain *films* were made by God or that specific software was coded by him. Imagine a future in which millions of our descendants murder each other over rival interpretations of *Star Wars* . . . Could anything—*anything*—be more ridiculous?" (*The End of Faith*, 35–6). As it happens the world we *are* living in is not that much less ridiculous than the one that Harris imagines. In our world, to give just one example, a woman received hundreds of rape and death threats just for making fun of *Star Wars* and its fans (Puvanenthiran, "Fox News Commentator"; Timpf, "I Will Not Apologize"). I am not saying that violent reactions to the mocking of a cherished cultural product automatically constitute "religious" behavior (I am also not saying they don't). My point is simply that commenters like Doniger and Harris dismiss much too casually, without evidence, the very possibility that there can be real congruency between fans of popular culture and adherents of religious traditions. This is a congruency addressed in some respects by all of the authors in this book, but it is examined most directly by Justin in chapter 7.

6

and the specific kinds of impacts involved, vary immensely and unpredictably. I am sure that Lucas never intended or imagined, for example, that as Dan and Joseph discuss below, *Star Wars* would provide inspiration for white supremacists. On the other end of the human rights spectrum many fans were overjoyed to have a female protagonist in *The Force Awakens*, and passionately protested Rey's absence from toys based on the film—an absence undoubtedly tied to her gender.[17]

These diametrically opposed responses to *Star Wars* by its fans—hateful and discriminatory versus liberal and inclusive—relate to the larger question of what the franchise teaches us about violence. Michelle Kinnucan, for example, argues that *Star Wars* is deeply problematic in this regard,

17. As evidenced from the tweet about action figures above, criticisms of Rey's absence from toys based on *The Force Awakens* sparked the hashtag #WheresRey (also #WhereIsRey). See Abrams, "J.J. Abrams"; Domonoske, "#WhereIsRey"; and McGinn, "Rey from *The Force Awakens*."

that it promotes "the myth of redemptive violence," the view that violence is not only necessary but salvific, that war must be waged before peace can obtain.[18] One example she offers to show how *Star Wars* is impacting the world with this myth involves men of U.S. Navy SEAL Team Six calling themselves The Jedi.[19] On the other hand, however, as Adnan points out in his chapter, the official doctrine of the International Church of Jediism involves affirmations that are fundamentally humane and peace-promoting:

> Jedi Believe:
>
> In the Force, and in the inherent worth of all life within it.
>
> In the sanctity of the human person. We oppose the use of torture and cruel or unusual punishment, including the death penalty.
>
> In a society governed by laws grounded in reason and compassion, not in fear or prejudice.
>
> In a society that does not discriminate on the basis of sexual orientation or circumstances of birth such as gender, ethnicity and national origin.
>
> In the ethic of reciprocity, and how moral concepts are not absolute but vary by culture, religion and over time.
>
> In the positive influence of spiritual growth and awareness on society.
>
> In the importance of freedom of conscience and self-determination within religious, political and other structures.
>
> In the separation of religion and government and the freedoms of speech, association and expression.[20]

John McDowell neatly summarizes the complexity of *Star Wars'* teachings on this subject: "the presentation of violence in the sets of narratives is not a simple one since this multi-part cultural product offers several forms of it. These forms range from something akin to a 'holy violence,' through more a sense of 'just war,' to an ethical philosophy approaching a full-blown redemptive 'non-violence.'"[21] The very different—sometimes contradictory—ways in which people use *Star Wars* in terms of violence should resonate strongly

---

18. Kinnucan, "Pedagogy of (the) Force."

19. Ibid., 69. This example comes from Gibson, *Warrior Dreams*, 285–6.

20. Temple of the Jedi Order, "Doctrine."

21. McDowell, *Identity Politics*, 6.

with questions that scholars and non-scholars alike often ask about more traditional religions. For example, how is it that some people who identify with a particular "world religion" (Buddhism, Christianity, Hinduism, Islam, Judaism) profess that pacifism, respect, and love for all people are core values of their tradition, while others who identify with the same religion hear a divine call to arms, a sacred demand to marginalize, oppress, or destroy those who are seen to pose a threat, or who perhaps are just different?

Of How and What

This question suggests another reason why scholars of religion might want to take *Star Wars* more seriously as an object of study: there are ways in which examining popular culture may facilitate greater flexibility in thinking about difficult or controversial issues such as violence. And the insights we arrive at may in fact also be applicable to religious traditions. That is to say, what we gain by turning our attention to works of popular culture and their fans is a(n apparent) lowering of the stakes, a release from worries about trampling on sacred orthodoxies. Which is not to say that we shouldn't be worried about such trampling, just that we likely wouldn't be; most people, in my experience, are much more hesitant making contentious proclamations about, say, the Bible, than they are about *The Empire Strikes Back*. Also, to be blunt: most scholars of religion themselves have, or had, religious convictions of their own. A struggle for many in this field, then, is to be as objective as possible regarding data about which they may have very strong personal convictions. If a religion scholar is also a Buddhist, it may be somewhat easier for them to be objective about Luke Skywalker than about Siddhartha Gautama.

As Michel Desjardins points out, how we approach our investigations is intimately tied to the data being considered: "our choice of *what* we study, when we study 'religion,' affects our notion of religion and especially the extent to which our beliefs and biases impact our research."[22] For those unfamiliar with the academic study of religion, the field includes several biases beyond the obviously religious ones. It has been much criticized, for example, for an over-emphasis on origins, on texts, on men. When we continue to focus the majority of our efforts on sacred writings—most frequently, the Bible—we reinforce these emphases.[23] Once we shift our object

22. Desjardins, "Religious Studies," 148.
23. Ibid., 148–51.

of study, though, some or all of these concerns fade significantly. In Michel's case[24] he began his career as a scholar of Gnosticism and the New Testament, but changed academic lanes entirely to think instead about religion and food. Doing so meant that both origins and texts became much less important: he was looking at what people do in the present, not what they wrote in the past. In addition, he notes:

> Similar points can be made about the role of women (and children). If we keep studying leaders, and writers of texts and rule books, we will find men, and more men. If we look for other ways in which religious life is nurtured—often in equally significant ways—women are everywhere; in fact, when looking at the vital role that food plays in people's religious lives the question sometimes becomes, where are the men? Women are minorities in only certain parts of religious life.[25]

As with food, the study of popular culture is inherently more present-focused, and less dominated by texts. In many cases, as with *Star Wars*, the emphasis is often still on men in terms of creators and protagonists; but when you turn to the fans, the ones who ensure that "religious life [of popular culture communities] is nurtured," then we find—as Michel did—that "women are everywhere."[26]

If *what* we study as "religion" impacts *how* we study it, then one final reason (that I will mention here) why looking at *Star Wars* and its fans could be helpful is that this approach might encourage us to take ourselves and our work less seriously in certain respects. As solemn and mythic as *Star Wars* is in many ways, and as serious as its fans are about it, one of

24. Although he is not one of the authors in this book Michel Desjardins and I have known one another for almost thirty years, which is why I'm using his first name. As a very young scholar at the University of Toronto in the late 1980s, he was one of my first religion professors. After I completed my undergraduate degree our families became friends, in part because we lived in the same west end Toronto neighborhood. We have eaten countless meals together, many at home. I have had snowball fights with his sons. It seems ridiculous to refer to him as "Desjardins."

25. Ibid., 154–55.

26. Thus Will Brooker, for example, states: "although *Star Wars* seems to have little to offer girls and women, it nevertheless enjoys a significant female fandom across several distinct communities, from the teen sites built around adoration for Luke Skywalker to an explicitly feminist project of reevaluation based on the argument that Boba Fett is female" (*Using the Force*, 9). In their chapters for this book, both Chris and Kutter similarly discuss various ways in which girls and women have always been passionately engaged *Star Wars* fans.

the reasons for the franchise's enduring appeal is that it is *fun*. It is fun on its own terms, and it is fun for people to play with. Which is to say, fans of course do not simply and passively receive meaning from *Star Wars*; they *create* it.[27] And they often have a really good time when they do. There are literally millions of examples of this phenomenon;[28] here are just two, both of which also happen to involve traditional notions of "religion." The first is a YouTube video by Nye Armstrong, an American Muslim and graphic designer, in which she shows viewers how to tie their hijab so it looks like Princess Leia's iconic hairstyle from Episode IV.[29]

27. One of the most influential studies of the ways in which fans actively participate in popular culture, rather than passively consume it, is Henry Jenkins' *Textual Poachers*. Not surprisingly, Jenkins' work is referenced by several authors in this book (Adnan, Justin, Ken, and Kutter).

28. In *Using the Force: Creativity, Community and Star Wars Fans*, Will Brooker identifies and discusses a wide range of creative responses to *Star Wars*, including websites, fiction, art, music, comics, and films. In the book's Preface, Brooker describes how he posted a notice to a *Star Wars* fan site asking people to email him a paragraph about why the films were important to them. He was instantly *flooded* with responses, which multiplied as he read them—he felt "like Mickey Mouse in *The Sorcerer's Apprentice*"—and in less than two hours Brooker asked the webmaster to remove his notice. He kept only the first one hundred responses, which ended up comprising the bulk of his research for the book (*Using the Force*, xiii). His experience with this website fits well with Henry Jenkins' assertion that *Star Wars* is exceptional in the degree to which it has inspired responses from fans ("*Quentin Tarantino's Star Wars*," 155–57)—although not, again, from religion scholars.

29. Armstrong, "Princess Leia Hijab Tutorial"; see also Peppers, "The Force is Strong."

The second example is of the *Star Wars*-themed wedding of Ronnie Fung and Janet Patterson on Toronto Island in June 2016. Unlike many similar weddings cosplay was not involved; instead, Janet's dress and Ronnie's bowtie both simply displayed the same R2-D2 print. The ritual included toy lightsabers and the officiant stating: "May the Force be with you."

Photo courtesy of Santiago Gomez.[30]

Of course as already mentioned not all fan responses to *Star Wars* are as positive as the ones above; some in fact are explicitly violent. Setting aside the vitriolic reactions, though, I'm left wondering: to the extent that *Star Wars* is fun, and (many of the) fan responses to *Star Wars* are fun, would it be a good thing if academics studying the films and/or the fans had fun doing so? Your mileage may vary, but my own answer to this question is a definite "yes."

Playfully Serious and Seriously Playful

It is my contention that taking ourselves less seriously would, for what it's worth, make us better human beings—along the lines of Steve Dallas putting aside his default sense of self-importance to help cheer up Sam. I

30. My thanks to Adnan for telling me about the *Star Wars*-themed wedding of his friends Janet and Ronnie, and for asking their permission to let me use their photo here. And my thanks to Janet and Ronnie (and the photographer, Santiago), for saying yes.

also think that being less serious in certain respects would make us better scholars. One point to this end refers back to the discussion above, about the trickiness of bracketing religious ideologies when studying specific traditions. In part the issue here is one of taking everything involved very, very seriously—arguably, too seriously to be fully neutral and scientific. As Michel, again, notes, when you study sacred texts "interpretations matter. They matter enormously, actually, since they have the possibility of significantly affecting a person's core beliefs and religious practice."[31] If we take the object of our study less seriously—if, say, we are looking at *Star Wars* rather than the Bible—we are perhaps more likely to be open to any number of interpretations, no matter how odd or even contradictory, should a reasonable case be made for them.[32]

---

31. Desjardins, "Religious Studies," 152.

32. A related point is that we would similarly benefit from adopting a more irreverent stance towards the work of other *scholars*, especially those with great and (more often than not) intimidating reputations. It is one thing to treat such work thoughtfully and respectfully; it is another to accept it as dogma and/or to use it as a rhetorical bludgeon to quiet dissenting views. Just as we need to be able to play with our data, we should be having some degree of responsible fun with the ideas of our academic peers and predecessors.

And as we stop regarding certain scholars as untouchable superstars, so should we also stop trying to *become* such stars ourselves. Ideally this approach will in turn lead to greater community and collaboration with our fellow academics and with those outside of academia—not to mention more frequent, meaningful, and transparent recognition of the community and collaboration that *already exists*. As Métis scholar Zoe Todd points out:

> In euro-american academia, the arts, media, politics, and literature we are enthralled, obsessed with two things: 'innovation' and individuality. The triumph of individual will to manifest something new new new trumps everything else. Granting agencies often focus on a single Principal Investigator to the exclusion of whole teams of human and more-than-human beings who make certain projects or ideas possible. News reporters want to find the new voice, the emerging voice, the singular representative of a community to demonstrate the raw will of a single body, mind, and spirit. They want us to believe that these achievements are not the product of the blood, sweat, and labour of myriad co-convenors, co-thinkers, collaborators, and co-dreamers who lift each other up in often dreary, cold, and impossible (impassible) academic systems and structures. They want us to believe that there is no village of academic aunties (as per Erica Violet Lee's brilliant terminology), sisters, cousins, kokums working insistently to make spaces for one another within the walls of academe and beyond. . . . Without these myriad relationships there could be no singular triumph. And without these relationships, the work we do would be pretty dull and dreary. ("Tending Tenderness")

One of the other ways in which popular culture pushes us to be more open, not only about our objects of study but about our own perspectives, is in how it plays with the world around us—which, according to Keith Booker, is especially true of science fiction:

> The ability to encourage us to rethink even our most entrenched notions about the world . . . is perhaps the central most important resource of science fiction as a cultural form. Because of the nature of science fiction as a genre, even a seemingly regressive work such as *Star Wars* asks us to imagine a world different from our own, an exercise that in itself forces us to adopt perspectives that are different from those we habitually inhabit.[33]

This very book contains opposing understandings of *Star Wars*. John, for example, suggests that the shift we see in *The Force Awakens* away from the simple good/evil dualism of the original trilogy reflects a more nuanced understanding of a morally complex world. Lindsay, in contrast, looks at the film through a Jungian lens and worries that, without a clear representative of the "dark side," neither the hero nor the viewer of the film is afforded the chance to integrate their own shadow and become psychologically whole. Booker himself offers competing understandings of the Rebel Alliance that are quite shocking yet entirely reasonable. Clearly the rebels are the heroes, coded as "American" in various ways.[34] However they are also, by many definitions, terrorists, waging an illegal war against the government. Booker even points out that Luke and Obi-Wan strongly resemble the members of Al-Qaeda: they "emerged from their desert homes,

---

33. Booker, *Alternate Americas*, 119. Booker also makes the point, related to my own above, that because works of popular culture are often not taken seriously they can explore a wide range of topics that otherwise might be problematic. Science fiction films, for example, "despite being widely regarded as mere entertainments, have often provided serious and thoughtful explorations of important contemporary social and political issues. Indeed, the very fact that genre films such as science fiction have generally not been taken as works of 'serious' cinema has sometimes allowed them a special freedom to address controversial topics" (ibid., 266).

34. In addition to most Rebels' American accents (in contrast to the Empire's largely British ones), Booker points to the Cold War allegory of *Star Wars*, with the Empire of course standing in for the Soviet Union (ibid., 116). The original trilogy also draws on various narrative tropes common in the U.S.: "Luke Skywalker, as the young prince coming of age . . . is a stock figure from Western fairy tales, just as Leia . . . is essentially the stereotypical damsel in distress, though one with considerable resources of her own. Han Solo is a stock figure from American film, especially Westerns, in which individualist loners . . . frequently become reluctant heroes when confronted by evil" (ibid.).

buoyed by their spiritual beliefs to think they can fight an opponent with vastly superior technological resources."[35]

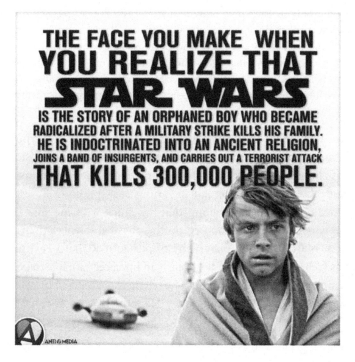

Source: http://theantimedia.org.

Aside from encouraging us to commit to particular interpretations when thinking about religion, seriousness has another, more general, academic drawback: it can lead us to place too much weight on arriving at conclusions that are considered "important" in some way, on coming up with grand explanatory theories. This focus can have a variety of negative effects, from creating a kind of research paralysis caused by performance anxiety, to (consciously or unconsciously) making data fit our theories rather than the other way around. In *Storytracking*, Sam Gill offers a powerful example of this latter problem as it concerns the ways in which ritual practices of the Arrernte, an Australian Aboriginal community, have been used for more than a century to fit the agendas of many different theorists of religion.[36] One such theorist is Mircea Eliade, identified by some as the most influen-

35. Ibid., 118.
36. Gill, *Storytracking*.

tial scholar in the field, who Gill argues was more concerned with his own ideas than with the reality of the Aborigines themselves:

> It is ironic that the only book that attempts a broad presentation of Australian aboriginal religions is Eliade's *Australian Religions*, a book written by a scholar who never visited the country, who spoke none of the languages, who probably never met an aborigine, who was uncritical of his sources, and who in the final analysis was interested in the Australians largely to demonstrate the reality of his generic understanding of religion.[37]

When we are playing, however, when we are having fun, the journey is absolutely more important than the destination. It's not the conclusions that matter, it's how we get to them. Which, in turn, makes the work itself both more enjoyable and less vulnerable to various corruptions.[38]

A story that makes this point that has stuck with me since I was a teenager, when I was more focused on the physical sciences than the human ones, is from the autobiography of physicist Richard Feynman. He describes feeling "burned out" fairly early in his career, unable to even start any research projects, in part because he felt he was expected to accomplish great things.[39] Then he had an epiphany. He thought:

37. Ibid., 210.

38. There is not space here to go into this issue in detail, but it is a critical one in academia. Over-attachment to results has a consistently negative effect on scholarship. One example of this phenomenon involves "Impact Factor" (IF), which is a measure of how often the average article in a particular academic journal is cited. The IF is a way of determining how "important" a journal is, and hence how important an article published in that journal must be. This in turn means that many scholars will attempt to get their work into journals with a high IF, as this achievement will ostensibly demonstrate the value of their work. But citations do not measure actual quality, and citation frequency can be artificially manipulated (some journals, for example, have been censured for encouraging authors to cite articles in that journal, thereby increasing their IF). Also, journals with a high IF tend to be older and more established, which means that they tend to represent more academically conservative research. Within the study of religion, for example, there is an enormous number of very highly regarded English language journals that focus on the Bible in its various forms; but there are less than a handful that publish work on religion and popular culture, all of which are relatively new and none of which has the prestige of the more traditionally-oriented publications. And as of this writing, in February 2018, there are no academic journals at all on religion and food. The system, in other words, is self-perpetuating and in many respects discourages new lines of inquiry: people do certain types of research because that's the type of research that people do. For detailed discussions of how using Impact Factors can harm research see Bosman, "Nine Reasons"; and Metze, "Bureaucrats."

39. Feynman, *Surely You're Joking*, 172.

16

Physics disgusts me a little bit now, but I used to *enjoy* doing physics. Why did I enjoy it? I used to *play* with it. I used to do whatever I felt like doing—it didn't have to do with whether it was important for the development of nuclear physics, but whether it was interesting and amusing for me to play with. When I was in high school, I'd see water running out of a faucet growing narrower, and wonder if I could figure out what determines that curve. I found it was rather easy to do. I didn't *have* to do it; it wasn't important for the future of science; somebody else had already done it. That didn't make any difference. I'd invent things and play with things for my own entertainment.[40]

Feynman recounts being in the school's cafeteria later that week and watching a plate wobble and spin when someone tossed it in the air. He became interested in the various motions of the plate, and started playing with calculations. When asked by one of his colleagues what the point of this work was, he replied: "There's no importance whatsoever. I'm just doing it for the fun of it."[41] That fun led Feynman to start thinking about atomic forces and electron spins, which in turn led to him receiving the Nobel Prize for discoveries in quantum electrodynamics. As he summarizes: "the whole business that I got the Nobel Prize for came from that piddling around with the wobbling plate."[42]

At the end of *Storytracking*, Gill suggests that one way of overcoming some of the key problems in the study of religion that he outlines in his book is to approach scholarship as "play."[43] By this he means, "a being at once of two minds or a holding at once of mutually exclusive positions."[44] There are a number of mutually exclusive positions he advocates that scholars simultaneously hold. One of the key tensions is between subjectivity and objectivity, between a recognition of our own situatedness, our tendency towards bias, and the desire for—and belief in the possibility of—arriving

40. Ibid., 173.

41. Ibid., 174.

42. Ibid.

43. Gill has been interested in the scholarly benefits of "play" for many years. In addition to his comments on the subject in *Storytracking*, he discusses it in detail in two further essays, "Play" (1998) and, twenty years later, "Play and the Future of the Study of Religion . . . and the Academy" (2009). In all three of these works Gill is clear that he is building his ideas from a foundation laid by Jonathan Z. Smith, most notably in his influential collection of essays, *Map is Not Territory: Studies in the History of Religions* (1978).

44. Gill, "Play," 451.

at conclusions that are objectively true.[45] A related tension is between the belief in our ability as scholars to help fill "the gaping chasm between the reality of our world and our understanding of it,"[46] and the humility to recognize not only that any contribution we make to this understanding might be wrong, but that academic over-confidence is deeply colonial and has historically been devastating to millions of people.[47]

Gill's stance fits closely with what I am advocating in this introduction. We need to simultaneously take ourselves seriously, doing our work responsibly and carefully, and not so seriously, avoiding the temptation to arrogance. Similarly we should recognize that popular culture often matters very deeply to people; at the same time, fans are able to have fun with it, to not take it seriously at all. George Lucas himself at different times has embraced this contradiction, seeing *Star Wars* both as a modern myth designed to teach people what it means to be good, while also declaring that it is "just a movie."[48] The idea of "play" can also apply to our academic interpretations, encouraging us not to worry about contradictory meanings but to "allow incongruities to stand."[49] Luke can be both hero *and* terrorist.

What I would add to Gill's understanding is the notion of play as *fun*. In the tensions he describes—between objectivity and subjectivity, confidence and humility—it is invariably the latter element we are missing, the one that depends upon not taking ourselves too seriously. One way to do that, as I have suggested, is to take some joy in what we do and why we do it, to have fun with our work as Feynman did.[50] In my own experience, for

45. As Gill states: "I have wanted to take seriously the shortcomings of a too quick and too pervasive objectivism without giving up the possibility of reading texts critically and decisively" (*Storytracking*, 214).

46. Ibid., 3.

47. Ibid., 215–16. In this respect, Gill calls for scholars to "break the cycle of achieving the *opposite* of what we always believe are highly laudable humane projects to help realize peace and understanding in the world" (ibid., 216; emphasis added). One of the most comprehensive studies of this phenomenon is Tomoko Masuzawa's *The Invention of World Religions*. Masuzawa demonstrates that European attempts from the nineteenth century onwards to understand "other" (non-Christian) religions were, no matter how commendably framed, projects of domination.

48. Block, "5 Questions."

49. Gill, *Storytracking*, 201.

50. It is important to point out that being less than entirely serious as a scholar does not come without professional risks. I once attended a talk on Gnosticism given by Michel Desjardins at the University of Toronto, which he began by playing a popular song and handing out figs (both the song and the figs were relevant to his topic). Immediately I heard

what it's worth, I have found that academics who are having fun more often than not make the best colleagues, scholars, and teachers.[51]

---

whispers of disdain from many of those around me, supposing that Michel's talk would be academically superficial before he had spoken a word, simply because he was doing something fun. I also know several young scholars who wanted to write about religion and popular culture but were strongly advised against it. The reason given was that such work would be looked upon unfavorably by more senior faculty members, and so hurt their chances at academic employment or promotion. And in fact, in 2014 when I went up for promotion to Associate Professor, the most damning comment I received about my file was a(n uninformed) critique of my use of popular culture in teaching.

These risks for junior scholars are increasingly significant, as the employment status of more and more university and college instructors has become increasingly precarious. The majority of these instructors have "adjunct" positions, which means they do not have permanent full-time employment—which in turn means they lack job security, benefits, and a fair wage. More often than not, in fact, adjunct professors live near or below the poverty line (Birmingham, "The Great Shame"). Institutions of higher education now depend, in other words, on systemic practices of exploitation. Kevin Birmingham discussed theses issues at length in the address he gave on receiving the 2016 Truman Capote Award for Literary Criticism. He also pointed out that when young/adjunct faculty are discouraged from taking risks, there are serious costs to the thing that universities often claim to value and support above all else: original, meaningful, research:

> The privilege of tenure used to confer academic freedom through job security. By now, decades of adjunctification have made the professoriate fearful, insular, and conformist. According to the AAUP [American Association of University Professors], adjunct faculty are about half as likely to undertake risky research projects, and the timidity moves up the ladder. "Professionalization" means retrofitting your research so that it accommodates the critical fads that will make you marginally more employable. It means cutting and adding chapters so that feathers remain unruffled. Junior faculty play it safe—conceptually, politically, and formally—because they write for job and tenure committees rather than for readers. Publications serve careers before they serve culture. ("The Great Shame")

51. This point applies, in my opinion, to all of the contributors to this book. John and I specifically sought out authors who were not only good scholars but also good people, who were not so self-serious, who had at least a little twinkle in their eyes. More than likely, as I have argued here, the simple fact that they were interested in writing about *Star Wars* at all meant that they likely did not take themselves seriously in unhelpful ways; it's a self-selecting group, as it were. As for John himself, one of the first things I was told about him many years ago, before we ever met, was that he had given a paper on *Star Wars* at the annual AAR meeting during which he imitated Yoda's voice. I immediately (and correctly) suspected that I would like him. He is in fact a wonderful person and a gifted, thoughtful scholar. He is also often quite funny, which I imagine contributes to his reputation as a skilled teacher. By this I do not simply mean that he is entertaining, but that humor can be a great tool for teaching religion (see Derry, "A Buddhist"; see also Gill, "Play as Pedagogy").

There are of course many ways to move ourselves towards less scholarly self-importance. We might introduce essays by discussing a comic strip; wear colorful bowties at conferences; give permission to colleagues to refer to us in publications by our first name; knit during academic presentations; serve Eggos at a scholarly panel; write a nonsensical footnote.[52] Again, there are serious reasons for such unseriousness, reasons that involve being accountable human beings as well as scholars, reasons not unconnected to comforting a sick child in the hospital. In this respect, we could definitely do worse than taking some measure of inspiration from Sith Lord Sexypants.

Bibliography

Abrams, Natalie. "J.J. Abrams: Lack of Rey Toys for Star Wars: The Force Awakens 'Preposterous.'" *Entertainment Weekly*. January 9, 2016. http://ew.com/article/2016/01/09/jj-abrams-star-wars-force-awakens-rey-toys.

Armstrong, Nye. "Princess Leia Hijab Tutorial." YouTube video, 9:03. Posted July 26, 2011. https://youtu.be/vhOGM2rdqKI.

Beavis, Mary Ann, et al. "The *Journal of Religion and Popular Culture*: More Than Old Wine in New Bottles." *Religion* 43:3 (2013) 421–33.

Birmingham, Kevin. "'The Great Shame of Our Profession': How the Humanities Survive on Exploitation." *Chronicle of Higher Education*. February 12, 2017. http://www.chronicle.com/article/The-Great-Shame-of-Our/239148.

Block, Alex Ben. "5 Questions with George Lucas." *The Hollywood Reporter*. February 9, 2012. http://www. hollywoodreporter.com/heat-vision/george-lucas-star-wars-interview-288523.

Booker, M. Keith. *Alternate Americas: Science Fiction Film and American Culture*. Westport: Praeger, 2006.

Bosman, Jeroen. "Nine Reasons Why Impact Factors Fail and Using Them May Harm Science." *I&M / I&O 2.0*. March 11, 2013. https://im2punto.wordpress.com/2013/11/03/nine-reasons-why-impact-factors-fail-and-using-them-may-harm-science.

Bowen, Jonathan L., and Rachel Wagner. "'Hokey Religions and Ancient Weapons': The Force of Spirituality." In *Finding the Force of the Star Wars Franchise: Fans, Merchandise, and Critics*, edited by Matthew Kapell and John Shelton Lawrence, 75–93. New York: Peter Lang, 2006.

Brooker, Will. *Using the Force: Creativity, Community and Star Wars Fans*. New York: Penguin, 2002.

Breathed, Berkeley. *Bloom County*. GoComics. http://www.gocomics.com/bloom-county.

Cowan, Douglas E. *Sacred Space: The Quest for Transcendence in Science Fiction Film and Television*. Waco: Baylor, 2010.

Daley-Bailey, Kate. "Star Wars and Religion." *Feeling the Force*. August 24, 2015. https://feelingtheforce.wordpress.com/2015/08/24/star-wars-and-religion.

---

52. Pickles.

Derry, Ken. "A Buddhist, a Christian, and an Atheist Walk into a Classroom: Pedagogical Reflections on Religion and Humor." *Bulletin for the Study of Religion* 42:3 (2013). https://journals.equinoxpub.com/index.php/BSOR/article/view/17914.

Desjardins, Michel. "Religious Studies that *Really* Schmecks: Introducing Food to the Academic Study of Religion." In *Failure and Nerve in the Study of Religion*, edited by William Arnal et al., 147–56. London: Equinox, 2012.

Domonoske, Camila. "#WhereIsRey? She's On Her Way, Says Hasbro." *npr.* January 6, 2016. http://www.npr.org/sections/thetwo-way/2016/01/06/462144156/-whereisrey-shes-on-her-way-says-hasbro.

Doniger O'Flaherty, Wendy. *Other People's Myths: The Cave of Echoes.* New York: Macmillan, 1988.

Feynman, Richard P. *"Surely You're Joking, Mr. Feynman!" Adventures of a Curious Character.* As told to Ralph Leighton. Edited by Edward Hutchings. New York: Norton, [1985] 1997.

Flotmann, Christina. *Ambiguity in Star Wars and Harry Potter: A (Post)Structuralist Reading of Two Popular Myths.* Bielefeld: Transcript, 2013.

Gibson, James William. *Warrior Dreams: Paramilitary Culture in Post-Vietnam America.* New York: Hill and Wang, 1994.

Gill, Sam. "Play." In *Guide to the Study of Religion*, edited by Willi Braun and Russell T. McCutcheon, 451–64. London: Cassell, 1998.

———. "Play and the Future of the Study of Religion . . . and the Academy." *Sam Gill: Body Dance Play.* July 2009. http://sam-gill.com/PDF/Play%20&%20Future.pdf.

———. "Play as Pedagogy." *Sam Gill: Body Dance Play.* February 10, 2009. http://sam-gill.com/PDF/Play%20and%20Pedagogy.pdf.

———. *Storytracking: Texts, Stories, and Histories in Central Australia.* New York: Oxford University Press, 1998.

Harris, Sam. *The End of Faith: Religion, Terror, and the Future of Reason.* New York: Norton, 2004.

Jenkins, Henry. "Quentin Tarantino's *Star Wars*?: Digital Cinema, Media Convergence, and Participatory Culture." In *Myth, Media, and Culture in* Star Wars: *An Anthology*, edited by Douglas Brode and Leah Deyneka, 153–67. Lanham: Scarecrow, 2012.

———. *Textual Poachers: Television Fans and Participatory Culture.* New York: Routledge, 1992.

Kapell, Matthew, and John Shelton Lawrence, eds. *Finding the Force of the Star Wars Franchise: Fans, Merchandise, and Critics.* New York: Peter Lang, 2006.

Kinnucan, Michelle J. "Pedagogy of (the) Force: The Myth of Redemptive Violence." In *Finding the Force of the Star Wars Franchise: Fans, Merchandise, and Critics*, edited by Matthew Kapell and John Shelton Lawrence, 59–72. New York: Peter Lang, 2006.

Lyden, John C. "Apocalyptic Determinism and *Star Wars*." In *Culture, Identities and Technology in the Star Wars Films: Essays on the Two Trilogies*, edited by Carl Silvio and Tony M. Vinci, 34–52. Jefferson: McFarland, 2007.

———. "Whose Film Is It, Anyway? Canonicity and Authority in *Star Wars* Fandom." *Journal of the American Academy of Religion* 80:3 (2012) 775–86.

Masuzawa, Tomoko. *The Invention of World Religions: Or, How European Universalism Was Preserved in the Language of Pluralism.* Chicago: The University of Chicago Press, 2005.

McDowell, John C. *The Gospel According to Star Wars: Faith, Hope, and the Force.* Louisville: Westminster John Knox, 2007.

————. *Identity Politics in George Lucas' Star Wars*. Jefferson: McFarland, 2016.

McGinn, Dave. "Rey from *The Force Awakens* Finally Makes Her Way to the Toy Shelf." January 14, 2016. *The Globe and Mail*. https://www.theglobeandmail.com/life/rey-from-the-force-awakens-finally-makes-her-way-to-the-toy-shelf/article28189973.

Metze, Konradin. "Bureaucrats, Researchers, Editors, and the Impact Factor—A Vicious Circle that is Detrimental to Science." *Clinics* 65:10 (2010) 937–40. https://www.ncbi.nlm.nih.gov/pmc/articles/PMC2972600.

Nietzsche, Friedrich. *Thus Spake Zarathustra: A Book for All and None*. Translated by Thomas Wayne. New York: Algora, [1891] 2003.

Peppers, Margot. "The Force Is Strong with This One! Girl Transforms Her Traditional Hijab into Princess Leia's Iconic Bun Hairstyle." *The Daily Mail*. August 14, 2013. http://www.dailymail.co.uk/femail/article-2392952/The-Force-strong-Girl-transforms-traditional-hijab-Princess-Leias-iconic-bun-hairstyle.html.

Porter, Jennifer. "'I Am a Jedi': Star Wars Fandom, Religious Belief, and the 2001 Census." In *Finding the Force of the Star Wars Franchise: Fans, Merchandise, and Critics*, edited by Matthew Kapell and John Shelton Lawrence, 95–112. New York: Peter Lang, 2006.

Puvanenthiran, Bhakthi. "Fox News Commentator Receives Death Threats for Star Wars Joke." *Sydney Morning Herald*. November 25, 2015. http://www.smh.com.au/entertainment/tv-and-radio/fox-news-commentator-receives-death-threats-for-star-wars-joke-20151125-gl7vid.html.

Rayment, Tim. "Master of the Universe." *Sunday Times Magazine*, May 16, 1999.

Seabrook, John. "Why is the Force Still With Us?" *The New Yorker*. January 6, 1997. http://www.newyorker.com/magazine/1997/01/06/why-is-the-force-still-with-us.

Temple Of The Jedi Order. "Doctrine of the Order." *Temple Of The Jedi Order: International Church of Jediism*. February 12, 2007. https://www.templeofthejediorder.org/doctrine-of-the-order.

Timpf, Katherine. "I Will Not Apologize for Making a Joke About *Star Wars*." *National Review*. November 24, 2015. http://www.nationalreview.com/article/427560/i-will-not-apologize-making-joke-about-star-wars-katherine-timpf.

Todd, Zoe. "Tending Tenderness and Disrupting the Myth of Academic Rock Stars." *Urbane Adventurer: Amiskwacî*. July 20, 2017. https://zoestodd.com/2017/07/20/tending-tenderness-and-disrupting-the-myth-of-academic-rock-stars.

ᵀᴴᴱ ᴹᴼᴿᴱ ᵀᴴᴵᴺᴳˢ ᶜᴴᴬᴺᴳᴱ

Historical Political Context and *The Force Awakens*

JOHN C. LYDEN

Abstract: This essay suggests that, even with the great similarities in plot and structure that exist between *The Force Awakens* and *A New Hope,* the reception of each by their original viewers differed due to the differences in their respective historical-political contexts, so that the films conveyed different meanings to their respective audiences. In particular, the easy dualisms of the earlier film have been problematized by the war on terror which has raised questions about the innocence of America in an increasingly complex world. Plot and character elements in *The Force Awakens* also convey an impression of flawed heroes and complex villains, none of whom is totally at fault nor free of blame, supporting the greater sense of moral and political ambiguity that many Americans now have. In the end, the political sensibilities of the viewers color what they see in the myth, which was as true of the original films as it is of the newer additions to the canon.

IT is now a commonplace to note that *The Force Awakens* replicates multiple elements of the original film, now known as *Episode IV: A New Hope,* which first appeared in theaters in 1977. These include not only the overarching narrative of a group of rebels' desperate attempt to stop an evil empire that is intent on controlling the galaxy by violence and intimidation, but individual elements of the original film (or the original trilogy) are also reproduced such as: crucial information is hidden in the memory banks of a droid, which must be kept from the Empire; an orphan on a desert planet is soon entrusted with the droid, though not knowing its contents, and is enlisted into the battle with the Empire; this orphan soon learns that she (in 1977, he) has a mysterious ancestry linked to Jedi skills which she can begin to develop; the enemy is a family member turned bad, whose father (and in 1983, the son) tries to get him to turn back from the dark side; a rebel planet is destroyed by an Imperial weapon, which can itself be destroyed by disabling the shield generator and attacking it with X-wing fighters which have to fly through trenches; and of course, as one IMDb reviewer (sonofhades) puts it, an "epic villain wears a mask that distorts his voice and sadly, looks better with the mask on than without it."[1]

Fan reactions to the film, positive or negative, were also largely based on whether they liked or disliked this resemblance to the original film. Looking at IMDb non-professional reviews—which admittedly is not a random sampling, but does show a group of dedicated fans willing to comment—out of about 4,000 reviews, most written within the first month of TFA's release, 28 percent "Loved it" and 70 percent "hated it." Here is a sample of the haters: "This movie is simply terrible. It has not depth at all. In the prequels with bad acting, terrible special effects and lack of real sets sucked yes, but at least they had a good story. The entire story is basically the original three films mashed together into 130 minutes of rehashed fan appeasement, no original story" (LiveFire1: sic). Or: "This felt like a parody" (TheForceWentBacktoSleep) and "The New 'New Hope' dies at the hands of the Disney Money-Making Machine" (elnaraniall). Or: "Star Wars is Dead. Bring back George Lucas! All is forgiven! Makes the prequels look like Masterpieces!" (magicbeatledel).[2]

And in contrast, there were those who loved it: "Yes, the plot and beats are VERY similar to A New Hope, but that was a great movie. If it ain't broke, don't fix it" (Guy2026). And to those who blame the film for too cautiously reproducing the original plot, one reviewer commented, "What happened last time somebody took a risk with the Star Wars Universe? The Prequels happened" (chaag-89951).[3] So the real difference between the lovers and haters isn't whether they thought it was original, but whether they liked that it wasn't, or were disappointed that it wasn't. It may also be that Disney and director J. J. Abrams decided on market caution in creating a

1. Reviews and Ratings, "Hated it."
2. Ibid.
3. Reviews and Ratings, "Loved it."

product so much like Episode IV in order to guarantee financial success. Notwithstanding some of the haters, the movie has done well: with a world-wide gross of over 2 billion dollars, this puts *TFA* at #3 of all time, right after *Avatar* and *Titanic*. And even adjusted for inflation, at this writing it is still in 11th place for the top domestic gross of all time.[4]

But if one looks at Box Office for all the *Star Wars* films, we don't see the prequels having done so much worse. They cost more to make, but all six of the first *Star Wars* films netted between 442 and 907 million US dollars after production costs. Noting that the average production cost of the prequel trilogy was 114 million as opposed to the average cost of the original films (20 million), and not adjusting for inflation, we can see a net box office profit (based on worldwide gross) of the 6 films, in millions of US dollars, in order of episodes I–VI as follows: 907, 534, 736, 764, 520, and 442. One can see that the prequels netted an average of 726 million USD as opposed to the original trilogy average of only 575 million, and that Episode I earned more than any of the others.[5] So there was no overriding financial reason to so precisely mimic the form of Episode IV in making VII. Why then the duplication?

Perhaps, apart from marketing concerns, there was a desire to return to the structure of Joseph Campbell's monomyth, which did provide the structure for the original storyline. As Campbell mapped it out in *The Hero with a Thousand Faces*, it includes these stages: the hero is called to an adventure, initially refuses it, receives supernatural aid, crosses the threshold of his or her world to enter the "belly of the whale," is proven worthy through various ordeals, confronts a father figure, and finally conquers the monster and is reconciled to the father.[6] I have elsewhere noted that there is much more going on in *Star Wars* than just the monomyth, as Lucas brought in a variety of religious, philosophical, political, and genre elements to construct *Star Wars*. I have also noted that Campbell's understanding of the

4. "All Time Box Office Top 100."

5. All this data is available at "Filmsite Movie Review: Star Wars Episode IV: A New Hope (1977)." Of course, one might adjust these numbers for inflation, which would mean that (adjusted to 2017 dollars) the profit in millions of the six films (in numerical order) would be 1331, 725, 922, 3082, 1543, and 1085. This puts the average of the original trilogy at 1902 as opposed to the 992 average for the prequels; this difference reflects the significant inflation that has occurred since the original films appeared. For example, four dollars today buys what one dollar did in 1977. One should also note that the cost of movies has not increased fourfold since then, which cuts the profit margin for more recent films when adjusting for inflation.

6. Campbell, *The Hero*.

monomyth is colored by his own philosophy. He psychologizes the nature of myth, as he is heavily influenced by Jung, and reduces the hero's journey to essentially a battle with one's own inner demons, which leads to a monistic realization that all is one; we embrace our shadow side and find that there is ultimately no distinction between self and God.[7] Political or historical action is then largely irrelevant to Campbell as it takes a back seat to the importance of personal psychological reintegration and self-discovery; there is no hope for redemption in the realm of history. Campbell did not view political action as very effective or as a realm of salvation; instead we must learn to live with conviction in our own times, regardless of the politics, as he pessimistically concluded that we probably cannot change them.[8]

I don't think *Star Wars* can be reduced to this philosophy, however, as there is clearly a transcendent Force and the possibility of redemption and forgiveness through our actions, as well as a real universe and real people, external to ourselves, that can be saved through our efforts—basically Christian categories, secularized, with some colonization of East Asian philosophy and religion thrown in for good measure. It also appears that politics actually matters in all the *Star Wars* films, as it is the primary theater for the conflicts that occur; it isn't just about personal integration.

If *Star Wars* has a political point to make, however, it may not be totally clear what it is. Michael Ryan and Douglas Kellner, in a study done in the early 1980s interviewing viewers of the original film, found that most (57 percent) believed that "being true to oneself" was the essential message of the film rather than any political content, and that there was no agreement about who might be the contemporary political analogue either for the Empire or the rebels. Either side of the conflict might be viewed as right-wing, or left-wing, depending on the viewer; 24 percent said the Empire was like right-wing dictators, and 12 percent saw it like communism; most didn't give it a political analogue. Similarly, 74 percent of those surveyed viewed the rebels as more like conservative freedom fighters than leftist rebels, and references were sometimes made to Nicaragua, as the war between the leftist Sandinistas and the right-wing Contras was in the news at the time. This is perhaps not surprising as communism was viewed as a threat by most Americans in that decade, and they probably agreed with the Reagan administration's support of the Contras, thus they would tend to identify the "good guys" in *Star Wars* with the anti-communist Contras.

7. Lyden, *Film as Religion*, 60–2.
8. Lawrence and Jewett, *The Myth*, 273.

This does not necessarily represent any overall consistent view of the politics of *Star Wars*, however, as the film was more often viewed as supporting "liberal values" than any other political view (30 percent of viewers); but that judgment by viewers was also dependent to some extent on their prior political alignments, as 76 percent of conservatives saw the film as politically conservative in message, whereas liberals were almost as likely to regard the film as liberal in message as conservative (43 percent vs. 46 percent).[9]

Even given the inconsistency of this data, Ryan and Kellner are at pains to argue that the film had an overall conservative thrust. Although they admit that the "struggle against tyranny does to a certain extent transcend political demarcations" (and indeed, don't we always view our opponents as tyrants, regardless of whether we are politically left, right, or center?) still they argue that

> in the historical context of the late seventies, the privileged meaning of the film ("being true to oneself") was likely to fuel a conservative rather than a liberal political and social agenda. For at that time what conservatives were promoting was an individualistic ethic which equated self-fulfillment with capital accumulation, and as conservatives succeed in the eighties in imposing that agenda and that ethic on U.S. society, "being true to oneself" would increasingly come to mean "going for it" and "saving one's own hide."[10]

This is indeed a bizarre interpretation of Episode IV, unless in their version Han Solo did not in fact go back to rescue Luke, but instead invested his reward money and made a killing in the market, like a good capitalist.

There is also a longstanding attempt to view *Star Wars* as fascist. Yes, the end scene of Episode IV does look like *Triumph of the Will*, but the films are also about rebels fighting a corrupt empire that appears much more fascist than they are. John Lawrence and Robert Jewett have argued that *Star Wars* has an essentially fascist message, but they do not make a completely convincing case for their view. They note the irrationalism and emotionalism of the Force, the role of charismatic heroes with special abilities, and their use of violence—but these do not define fascism. Benito Mussolini, who should know, defined fascism by three things: "Everything in the state" (i.e., total conformity to it is demanded); "Nothing outside the State" (as the fascist nation is destined to rule a world empire, all other

9. Ryan and Kellner, *Camera Politica*, 234–45.

10. Ibid., 235.

27

nations must submit); and "Nothing against the State," meaning no one is allowed to question the state, so censorship of opposing views is required.[11] The Rebels do not have these characteristics to their ideology, but the Empire does. It is likely, then, that Americans would identify with the rebels as foes of totalitarianism, such as that of the Soviet Union, which was in full sway at the time.

The tendency to equate *Star Wars* with conservative values without evidence dates back to the time of the original film. In 1978, Andrew Gordon was among the first to suggest that the appeal of the mythic forms of *Star Wars* related to the political context of the times:

> We are in a period in which the heroes have been cast down through such national catastrophes as Vietnam and Watergate, when the lines between good and evil grow cloudy, and when sexual identities have been redefined by the women's movement. Meanwhile, we have created a machine world for ourselves, a world that seems drained of spiritual values, a world in which we feel impotent and alien. We desperately need a renewal of faith in ourselves as Americans, as good guys on the world scene, as men and women, as human beings who count, and so we return to the simpler patterns of the past.[12]

Gordon does not explicitly say whether this is a good or a bad thing, but he regards it as axiomatic that we need faith in ourselves as Americans, as good guys, with clear dualisms of right and wrong such as appear in *Star Wars*. This is an aspect of the doctrine of American Exceptionalism which was under siege at the time, due to what George H. W. Bush later called the "Vietnam Syndrome," referring not to the war itself but to the way the media covered it and the way Americans saw it, as a failure, leading Americans to reject the notion that America can have successful wars and demonstrate its role as a world leader. Bush said we had "kicked the Vietnam Syndrome once for all" after victory in the Persian Gulf War was declared in 1991 after a mere *seven weeks* of combat.[13] In any case, in 1977 Americans had lost a lot of faith in their government due to Vietnam and Watergate, and the "women's movement" (as Gordon calls it) was and is still paradoxically blamed for a loss in traditional values that supposedly require reinstating, as if the quest for freedom and equal treatment and

11. Mussolini, "The Doctrine."

12. Gordon, "*Star Wars*," 82.

13. Bush, "Remarks."

justice for all was somehow not tied to traditional American values. This sort of reactionary rhetoric was in its ascendancy as we entered the Reagan years; but the question remains whether the success of *Star Wars* was due in part to cashing in on these tendencies, and whether it appealed to those tendencies wittingly or unwittingly, or whether it was simply hijacked in support of them, as when Reagan nicknamed the Strategic Defense Initiative "Star Wars" technology.[14]

This is a question worth asking, because people have a habit of putting their own political spin on *Star Wars* that relates to their own historical and political context, giving it the meaning they want it to have to confirm their own worldviews. This again suggests one way in which *Star Wars* is like a sacred text, as true believers are always happy to engage in eisegesis to impose whatever meaning they wish on their Scriptures in support of their own ideology. And although politically biased webpages do not demonstrate mainstream American views for the most part, their views of *Star Wars* are informative if we are looking at some of the ways the films might be interpreted politically. Conservative Jonathan Witt liked *The Force Awakens* as it eschews what he sees as the leftist utopianism of the original trilogy in favor of a conservative Realpolitik that sees political evil as ineradicable and basic to history. He argues that it was a lack of leadership in the liberal Republic that allowed totalitarianism to return in the form of the First Order, suggesting that the naïveté of liberals prevents them from dealing with political evil strongly enough.[15] Mytheos Holt, in *The Federalist*, goes so far as make the conservative argument that the First Order should be seen as the good guys, as they bring order to the chaotic mess created by the liberal New Republic, and their strong arm tactics (including genocide and torture) are therefore legitimate.[16] In both cases, the return of evil is regarded as inevitable, and a strong show of force is needed to keep it in check. This implies hawkish support for the war on terror that blames soft liberals for the ascendancy of ISIS.

On the opposite side of the political spectrum, Chris Burnett in *Counterpunch* agrees that the war between the First Order and the Republic resembles that between ISIS and the US, but he does not agree that the film provides a legitimate argument in support of our own hawkish responses to conflict, or that the softness of liberals created ISIS *or* the First Order.

14. "The Strategic Defense Initiative."

15. Witt, "Wow!"

16. Holt, "The First Order."

Rather, he finds *The Force Awakens* at fault in its failure to provide political context for the rise of the First Order, and also he criticizes the film for attempting (however mistakenly) to legitimize a strong hawkish response to conflict without any moral or political limits.

> US citizens are always portrayed as innocent victims in support of truth and justice, and that their government is benevolent and full of good intent. Today, as a case in point, the dominant narrative is that ISIS came out of nowhere and has nothing to do with the US invasion of Iraq, or its policies in the Middle East. . . . In a similar fashion, the Rebels in *The Force Awakens* are always innocent victims responding to an outside Evil of great magnitude. Except today, that great Evil isn't fascist states hell bent on world domination, they are rogue nihilists Attacking Us For Our Freedoms.[17]

This is how most Americans have viewed terrorism since 9/11, Burnett claims, as a random nihilistic force that "hates our freedoms," and so they are unable to see how American political actions have contributed to the development of terrorism. Whether the Republic is similarly to blame for the First Order in the world of *Star Wars* is a moot point, Burnett argues, as the film operates to authenticate our own war on terror without taking any responsibility for how we have contributed to it.[18] Burnett admits that the context for viewing this today, in the midst of an endless war on terror which is used to justify our military interventionism, is very different from the historical context of the US in 1977, so that even if it is the same film in essence, it now has a different message because of the different historical context in which it is received. In another leftist analysis, Ian Millhiser at *ThinkProgress* argues that the dissolution of the Republic and its inability to govern the galaxy after Episode VI show the inevitable consequences of regime change, for just as the US has failed to bring peace to Iraq and Afghanistan but has only destabilized the region, so the Republic fails to bring peace to all, suggesting the dangers of interventionism.[19]

All these analyses, conservative or liberal, seem willing to identify the First Order with ISIS and the Republic with the US; they differ on what led to the First Order's (or ISIS's) development, whether it was liberal softness or neo-conservative interventionism, and what lesson we are to learn from that, even though this is not a question addressed at all in the film. In any

17. Burnett, "Why."
18. Ibid.
19. Millhiser, "The Writers."

case, there is a tendency to equate the political chaos seen in *The Force Awakens* with our current situation of global uncertainty and terrorism. And the vision of Episode VII is in fact a darker vision than that of Episode IV, since things have gotten this bad this quickly after the victory of the Rebel Alliance in Episode VI. This impression is aided by the fact that the source of much evil is the son of central characters Han and Leia, and watching Kylo Ren kill his father is rather traumatic for viewers who know Han as a beloved character played by a popular actor. We also see the extent of chaos in the film in the fact that Luke is somewhat inexplicably hiding, not very responsible behavior for a Jedi, and Han also abandoned the Republic and his family to go back to smuggling, which is hardly appropriate behavior for a war hero. There is also moral ambiguity in the new character of Finn, as a former stormtrooper who wrestles with guilt about his past; and Rey also has a difficult history, as she was abandoned by her family to live totally on her own in abject poverty as a scavenger, and is haunted by mysterious visions from which she seeks escape.

None of this sort of dark ambiguity of character was present in Episode IV, or even most of the original trilogy. It can then be seen not only that the external political context of the times differs from four decades ago, but the film itself differs in mirroring to a greater extent the ambiguity and complexity we increasingly see in our times, including the persistence of political evil, the difficulty of easy solutions, and even the morally compromised nature of some of our heroes. Conservatives think the movie is conservative because it shows we will always have evil enemies; liberals think it is liberal because it shows our own side as morally imperfect. But perhaps *The Force Awakens* has actually escaped some of the simplistic dualism of the original films just by offering a more complex universe, which while it might sanction the war on terror for some, critiques it for others. The meaning is in the eyes of the viewer. Yet we view this film in a different century with a different set of political issues than we had in 1977. This fact will inevitably affect how it is interpreted, even though no single meaning can be easily given to its mythic structure. Myths are opaque entities that resist interpretation, instead offering themselves as ciphers to decode, or think-pieces to encourage our reflection on our own values, goals, and destinies. Yes, it's just a *Star Wars* movie; but given how much heat the debates about it generate, and given the extent of the fandom, we would be wise not to dismiss it either as an important site of cultural self-reflection or as a reflection of who we are, and who we might become.

Bibliography

"All Time Box Office Top 100." *Filmsite*. http://www.filmsite.org/boxoffice.html.

Burnett, Chris. "Why Star Wars: 'The Force Awakens' is a Parable that Supports US Empire." *Counterpunch*, December 21, 2015. http://www.counterpunch.org/2015/12/21/why-star-wars-the-force-awakens-is-a-parable-that-supports-us-empire.

Bush, George H.W. "Remarks to the American Legislative Exchange Council." March 1, 1991. *The American Presidency Project*. http://www.presidency.ucsb.edu/ws/?pid=19351.

Campbell, Joseph. *The Hero with a Thousand Faces*. Princeton, NJ: Princeton University Press, 1972.

Gordon, Andrew. "*Star Wars*: A Myth for Our Time." In *Screening the Sacred: Religion, Myth, and Ideology in Popular American Film*, edited by Joel W. Martin and Conrad E. Ostwalt, 73–82. Boulder, CO: Westview, 1995. Originally published in *Literature/Film Quarterly* 6:4 (Fall 1978) 314–26.

"Filmsite Movie Review: Star Wars Episode IV: A New Hope (1977)." *Filmsite*. http://www.filmsite.org/starw.html.

Holt, Mytheos. "The First Order Are the (Anti-)Heroes of 'The Force Awakens.'" *The Federalist*, December 22, 2015. http://thefederalist.com/2015/12/22/the-first-order-are-the-anti-heroes-of-the-force-awakens.

Lawrence, John Shelton, and Robert Jewett. *The Myth of the American Superhero*. Grand Rapids: Eerdmans, 2002.

Lyden, John. *Film as Religion: Myths, Morals, and Rituals*. New York: NYU Press, 2003.

Millhiser, Ian. "The Writers Of 'Star Wars: The Force Awakens' Understand Regime Change Better Than George W. Bush." *ThinkProgress*, December 21, 2015. https://thinkprogress.org/the-writers-of-star-wars-the-force-awakens-understand-regime-change-better-than-george-w-bush-3fd5e1cb284b#.5flh6rxuc.

Mussolini, Benito. "The Doctrine of Fascism." 1932. *World Future Fund*. http://www.worldfuturefund.org/wffmaster/Reading/Germany/mussolini.htm.

Reviews and Ratings for *Star Wars: Episode VII, The Force Awakens*, "Hated it." *IMDb*. Accessed June 9, 2017. http://www.imdb.com/title/tt2488496/reviews?filter=hate.

Reviews and Ratings for *Star Wars: Episode VII, The Force Awakens*, "Loved it." *IMDb*. Accessed June 9, 2017. http://www.imdb.com/title/tt2488496/reviews?filter=love.

Ryan, Michael, and Douglas Kellner. *Camera Politica: The Politics and Ideology of Contemporary Hollywood Film*. Bloomington, IN: Indiana University Press, 1988.

"The Strategic Defense Initiative (SDI): Star Wars." *The Cold War Museum*. http://www.coldwar.org/articles/80s/SDI-StarWars.asp.

Witt, Jonathan. "Wow! J. J. Abrams Smuggles 3 Conservative Truths Out of Liberal Hollywood and Into #StarWars 7." *The Stream*, December 19, 2015. https://stream.org/star-wars-force-awakens-3-conservative-truths.

CHAPTER 2

THE BRIGHTEST SHADOW

From Fighting Darkness to Seeking It

LINDSAY MACUMBER

Abstract: This essay explores whether Darth Vader (in both the original and prequel trilogies) and Kylo Ren (in *The Force Awakens* and *Bloodline*) exemplify Joseph Campbell's (and Carl Jung's) shadow archetype. Kylo Ren arguably does *not* provide us with a satisfactory shadow figure, which could mean one of two things: either he is not the shadow, and we can look forward to another villain; or he is the shadow, but a very disappointing one. This latter possibility has extreme consequences since Campbell asserts that the confrontation and assimilation of the shadow by the hero is essential not only for their successful journey, but also for allowing us, as individuals invested in this myth, to successfully navigate the transitions and transformations in our lives.

Myth and Personal Transformation

Joseph Campbell's seminal studies of mythology argue not only that myths are characterized by a universal structure and archetypes, but also that they have a universal function. Incorporating Jung's work, Campbell argues, "It has always been the prime function of mythology and rite to supply the symbols that carry the human spirit forward, in counteraction to those other constant human fantasies that tend to tie it back."[1] Thus, the hero's journey is meant to symbolize the transformations (conscious and

---

1. Campbell, *The Hero*, 11.

unconscious) that all human beings must undergo in order to live successful, well-balanced, and mentally healthy lives.

In the best cases, failure to effectively experience these transitions can lead to an inescapable feeling that we have missed something in our lives, that we are somehow not on the right path or have missed our "calling." In the worst cases, it can lead to neurosis associated with not having successfully navigated the different phases of life, from childhood to adulthood.[2] The urgency to effectively navigate these phases is attested to not only by the universal nature of myth, but also by the fact that in the absence of myth (or a meaningful myth for the individual), other sources, such as psychoanalysis and popular culture, provide the means that help human beings experience and undergo their own calls to adventure, initiation, and return.[3]

The Mythic Archetypes and the Shadow

One of the primary ways in which myths help to "carry the human spirit forward," according to Campbell and Jung, is by presenting a series of characters, or archetypes, that represent aspects of the persona that are repressed and unintegrated into the consciousness.[4] In encountering these externalized (usually personified) aspects, the hero is able to confront and integrate the archetypes throughout their journey. Perhaps the most important of these archetypes, and also the most difficult to integrate, is the shadow. The shadow is also usually the easiest archetype to recognize, as it takes the form of the villain, the ultimate foe or nemesis of the hero that needs to be defeated if the hero is to complete their journey.

In reality, this externalized version of the shadow represents the aspects of the hero that are buried the deepest: they are nestled into the dark recesses of the unconscious, "the blind spot in your nature," "the backside of your light side."[5] Thus, in confronting the shadow, the hero is really confronting themselves, and also unearthing the "other side" of their potential. For this reason, the goal is not really to defeat the shadow, but to assimilate it, to embrace it.[6] What the hero seeks is an authentic confronta-

2. Campbell, *The Hero*, 11.
3. Campbell, *Pathways to Bliss*, 131–32.
4. Jung, *The Archetypes*, 5.
5. Ibid., 73.
6. Ibid., 80 and 40.

tion and mature assimilation of these previously unrecognized (although dark) aspects of themselves. In doing so, they unlock their full potential. The danger, of course, is that confronting the shadow can also lead to being consumed by it.

Darth Vader as Shadow: Episodes IV–VI

Because we know that George Lucas wrote episodes IV–VI in consideration of the monomyth,[7] it should not surprise us that the main villain, Darth Vader, corresponds to the shadow archetype perfectly. In the original trilogy, we see the hero and the shadow as two separate characters, Luke Skywalker and Darth Vader. This definite distinction between hero and shadow, good and bad, dark and light, creates what seems at first to be a highly dualistic universe. Overall, the original trilogy contains much less ambiguity about good and evil than we find in the prequels and *The Force Awakens*. The fact that the light and the dark result from the dual potentials of the Force is downplayed in favor of a dualistic, black and white universe.

Even though the original trilogy represents the hero and shadow as two distinct characters, it is possible to find indications that in confronting Darth Vader, Luke is really confronting his own shadow. Perhaps the most striking of these is, of course, the revelation that Darth Vader is his father, which forces Luke to realize "that he and his opposite are not of differing species but of one flesh."[8] We also see traces of this throughout Luke's training. On more than one occasion, Yoda warns him of the dangers of his impatience and anger, suggesting that even our hero is imbued with the characteristics that drive our shadow. In addition, when Luke enters the Cave of Evil (otherwise known as the Dark Side Cave),[9] a space that contains a projection, or representation, of his worst fears, he does in fact encounter Darth Vader. However, after defeating and decapitating this apparition in a lightsaber duel, the shadow's helmet explodes, revealing none other than our hero's face.[10]

---

7. Gordon, "*Star Wars*," 78.

8. Campbell, *The Hero*, 108.

9. This is what the cave is called on the *Wookiepedia* page, "Cave of Evil." In *The Empire Strikes Back*, Yoda only tells Luke that the cave is "strong with the dark side of the Force," and "A domain of evil" that contains "only what you take with you."

10. *The Empire Strikes Back*, 1:04:35–1:05:37.

Darth Vader's ultimate redemption can be interpreted as the result of Luke's success in confronting the shadow by acknowledging its identity as his father, and therefore, as a part of himself: "Luke does not try to escape his destiny. He knows that his life is linked with his father's. But instead of accepting his fate and joining the Sith, Luke chooses to use his connection with Darth Vader to bring his father back to the light side of the Force."[11] It is therefore Luke's commitment to his relationship with the shadow that moves Darth Vader to save Luke's life and fulfill the prophecy by killing the Emperor and restoring balance to the Force. What really signifies Darth Vader's redemption, however, is his removal of his helmet in order to show his face to his son. Because, as we shall see in the following section, this helmet represents Anakin's shadow that had consumed him, removing it allows Anakin and Luke to truly encounter one another, an encounter that signals Luke's success in confronting and assimilating his shadow.

Darth Vader as Shadow: Episodes I–III

While the shadow appears as an external archetype in the original trilogy, the prequels allow us to see what this journey looks like when the shadow is represented as an internal foe, as the dark side within the hero. Because the struggle is now between Anakin Skywalker and the (yet unrealized) Darth Vader, two aspects or potentialities of the same person, the understanding of good and evil in this trilogy is much less dualistic. Instead, we see the full range of possibilities inherent in the Force itself, which, like Anakin, contains both darkness and light. Thus, Anakin's "most essential trait is his ambiguity, his oscillation between the poles of good and evil and the closely related extremes of free will and determination."[12]

11. Last, *Star Wars*, 85.
12. Flotmann, *Ambiguity*, 145.

Anakin's embodiment of both darkness and light is represented visually in *Revenge of the Sith*.

The degree to which this ambiguity characterizes Anakin is made strikingly apparent in the story of his conception. As we learn from his mother, Shmi, Anakin has no human father. His conception is the result of a high level of midi-chlorians. In other words, he is born of pure Force energy. This implies not only that the Force is unusually strong in him, but also that it will take extra training from his mentors to ensure that he does not succumb to the dark side. However, because Anakin begins his Jedi training quite late, it seems unlikely that he will succeed in achieving this balance.

This is confirmed by the Jedi Council, particularly Yoda, who, upon meeting young Anakin, fears that he has already formed too many attachments (particularly to his mother), and is ruled by emotions, particularly fear, which lead to the dark side. Qui-Gon is the only one who seems to think Anakin's training is a good idea. Even Obi-Wan, who eventually takes on Anakin's training as a final promise to Qui-Gon, wonders why he can't sense that the boy is dangerous. Although the Council finally agrees to allow Obi-Wan to train Anakin, Yoda continues to fear that his training is a mistake, despite the possibility that "The Chosen One, the boy may be."[13]

As Anakin grows up this ambiguity grows with him. As is perhaps to be expected from a teenager who senses his potential for power, he is arrogant. He knows that he wants more than he should, and struggles to balance his longing for power with his training, "I'm not the Jedi I should

13. *The Phantom Menace*, 2:06:52.

37

be. I want more, and I know I shouldn't."[14] He begins to suspect that the Jedi are holding him back, not allowing him to reach his full potential, which, of course, would involve a confrontation with his shadow, or the dark side. Most significantly, he continues to be ruled by emotions and attachment. These are what lead him to secretly marry Padmé, to kill all the Tusken Raiders who hold his mother captive (including the children), and ultimately to seek the power to save Padmé's life. Anakin's decision to embrace his shadow is thus based on fear, the fear of losing his wife, just as Yoda predicted.

This embrace of his shadow, does not, however, lead to the balance of Anakin's light and dark sides. Instead of confronting and assimilating his shadow, Anakin is consumed by it. This is particularly apparent when, having agreed to become Senator Palpatine's apprentice, he kills an entire class of Jedi younglings.[15] In addition, when Anakin becomes convinced that Padmé has betrayed him by bringing Qui-Gon on her ship to confront him, he uses his power to put her in a Force choke (which becomes his signature hold), placing her life, which his turn to the dark side was to protect, in danger.[16] It is not, however, until Anakin puts on his dark side armor, particularly the helmet, that his transition is complete. There is perhaps no scene more iconic and anticipated in the entire series than the first assisted breath Anakin takes through his new life-support system. From this point on, or at least until he redeems himself and removes his helmet, he is known only as Darth Vader.

Kylo Ren as Shadow?

Whether Darth Vader is represented as an internal or external shadow, his presence in the myth of *Star Wars* is essential for the journeys and transformations of our heroes. His opposition to the hero is what allows us (the viewers, or participants in the myth), to navigate our own life journeys, and successfully move through the transitions and transformations our lives necessitate. It is for these reasons that the absence of a shadow figure in *The Force Awakens* is so unsettling. In fact, every aspect of our new villain, Kylo Ren, as revealed both in the film and in the novel *Bloodline* (which takes place before *TFA*), suggests that he does not conform to this archetype.

14. *Revenge of the Sith*, 53:19–26.
15. Last, *Star Wars*, 30.
16. Ibid., 62.

Unlike Anakin, who is born of pure Force energy and whose journey is a struggle to balance both sides of his inherent potential, Ren, or should I say, Ben Solo, is the child of two heroes. The legacy of this parentage is reflected in the fact that he is Obi-Wan "Ben" Kenobi's namesake. It is this legacy, and not any external or internal shadow, or even a hero, that becomes his primary nemesis in the film. Unlike Luke, who fought against an external(ized) shadow, and Anakin, who fought the darkness within himself, Ren struggles against the goodness, he fights the power of the light. He wants (desperately) to be the shadow his grandfather was, and even wishes to surpass his legacy, understanding his ultimate redemption as his fatal flaw.[17] Despite his commitment to this goal, however, he is unable to shake his goodness; the pesky light keeps intruding. The primary conflict we see in the film is therefore not between a hero and a shadow, but between Ren's aspirations for darkness and his inherent goodness.

This does not necessarily mean that Ren only does good things or that he is a hero figure himself. After all, we know that he kills all the young Jedi training alongside him with Luke, and also his own father. However, even these two evil deeds, which would seemingly signify his initial and final transition to the dark side, or consummation by his shadow, can be interpreted as failed attempts at extinguishing his inherent goodness.

Because we only see Ren's murder of those training alongside him in Rey's vision (when she touches Anakin's lightsabre), we don't really learn why he perpetrates this deed. *Bloodline* provides some clues here, revealing, or at least suggesting, that this action is Ben's response to learning that Darth Vader is his grandfather. This closely guarded secret, which was previously only shared by Leia, Han, Luke, and probably Chewbacca, is revealed publicly to the Galactic Senate by one of Leia's political rivals in an attempt to discredit her. This public revelation forces Leia to record a private message for Ben, hoping it reaches him before the news. We never find out whether it does, and so we can only speculate as to whether Ben's reaction would have been different if it had.

Based on this information, it seems plausible to conclude that Ren is compelled to kill Luke's trainees and become Snoke's apprentice because he is confronted with the secret of his family heritage, and perhaps even that this allows him to acknowledge a darkness within himself that he always sensed. This interpretation seems confirmed when Han attempts to comfort Leia, who worries they made the wrong decision by sending him away

17. Hidalgo, *Star Wars*, 26.

to train with Luke, by telling her there is nothing they could have done to change his fate, since, "there's too much Vader in him."[18] However, in the extra features of *The Force Awakens*, Adam Driver suggests that Ben's actions can instead be understood as resulting from a deep sense of abandonment by his parents, who had very little involvement in his life after they sent him away for training: "If you really imagine the stakes of him, in his youth, having all these special powers, and having your parents kind of be absent during that process on their own agendas, equally as selfish. He's lost in the world that he was raised in and feels that he was kind of abandoned by the people he's closest with. He's angry because of that, I think, and he has a huge grudge on his shoulders."[19] Thus, this evil deed, which seems to signify his initial turn to the dark side, may not be motivated by an embracing of his shadow, but by a sense of abandonment.

Once Ren becomes Snoke's apprentice, the First Order issues a decree indicating that his birth name never be spoken.[20] This is an attempt to demonstrate that Ren's ties to his previous life, which was characterized by his family legacy and his Jedi training, are broken, and that he is now fully committed to the dark side and the command of the Knights of Ren. Nevertheless, even his adopted name, Kylo, which is a composite of Skywalker and Solo, suggests that this transition is not in fact complete. This is further evidenced by Ren's actions and motivations throughout the film, which demonstrate that despite his best efforts, he continues to be overcome by the light. We see this especially in his pleading with his grandfather's memory, here represented by his helmet (which, significantly, represents Anakin's shadow), for guidance in defeating the light he feels continually "pulling" him.[21] It could also be argued that Ren's failure to interrogate Rey, who is just discovering her Force power, is due to his inability to embrace the power of the dark side, and thus benefit from its power.

When Ren kills his father it seems that this signifies his success in confronting his shadow, or turning to the dark side. The importance of this act for his personal transformation is indicated by his dialogue with Snoke, who tells Ren, "Even you, master of the Knights of Ren, have never faced such a test." Confident in his ability to "pass" this test, Ren replies, "By the grace of your training, I will not be seduced." He, of course, is

18. *The Force Awakens*, 1:24:22.

19. Driver on Kylo Ren in *Secrets of* The Force Awakens.

20. Hidalgo, *Star Wars*, 24.

21. *The Force Awakens*, 59:07.

talking about being seduced by the light (unlike both Luke and Anakin). Even Snoke, however, seems to doubt his resolve: "we shall see," he replies, "we shall see."[22]

When Ren meets his father and is confronted with this task, Han tries to appeal to the goodness he knows is still present (in fact, I would argue, dominant) in his son. Importantly, the first thing Han asks of Ren is that he remove his mask (helmet) so that he can see "the face of my son." Although Ren insists that his son, or Ben, is gone, he does admit that he "is being torn apart," that he knows what he has to do but not if he has the strength to do it. This could mean that he knows he needs to kill his father in order to embrace his shadow; or, it could mean that he needs to leave with his father, "go home," and no longer serve as Snoke's apprentice.[23] Because he kills Han, it seems that it is the former that is the case, that the light that Ren has been fighting all along may finally let go of its hold on him, and we may finally have a formidable shadow.

It is significant, after all, that this test occurs just moments before the final armed conflict between Rey and Ren. The connection between these two scenes is further emphasized by the fact that the wound that Chewbacca inflicts upon Ren after he kills Han becomes instrumental in this battle. Not only is it made apparent that Ren is wounded, as his blood stains the white snow on which they duel, but it also serves as an indication that Ren has not, in fact, successfully embraced his shadow and transitioned to the dark side. This becomes apparent as every time Ren has a reprieve from direct fighting, he strikes his wound in order to fuel the pain, anger, and hatred, and therefore tap into the dark side powers that might allow him to defeat Rey. The fact that he needs to resort to this strategy, rather than simply taking advantage of the new dark-side powers he received from his father's murder, indicates that his transition is not complete.

It should also be noted that in this final battle, Ren is unable to use his power to summon his grandfather's lightsaber to him, a feat that Rey accomplishes fairly effortlessly. The implication is not only that Ren has not embraced his shadow, but also that Rey, our hero who is just discovering her Force powers, has already tapped into the ambiguity of the Force more effectively than her opponent. This understanding is also supported by the fact that, although they do not complete their battle, there is no clear winner or loser. Thus, although it is Rey's first time fighting with a saber, she

22. *The Force Awakens*, 49:20–51:10.
23. *The Force Awakens*, 1:45:01–1:48:22.

proves herself a formidable hero and opponent, even when faced with Ren's years of training.

What all of this amounts to is the fact that if Ren is our shadow, he is a very disappointing one indeed. We see this disappointment in Rey's face the moment he takes off his helmet to reveal what one reviewer calls the face of "a teen who's borrowed dad's car without telling him."[24] This reaction was shared by many fans and reviewers, who expressed "incredulity that this pallid, clean-shaven dude was the most menacing figure in the Star Wars universe."[25] Even Emilio Ranzato, film critic for the Vatican's newspaper, *L'Observatore Romano*, claims that in comparison to "the two most-efficient villains," of the original trilogies, Kylo Ren falls quite short. Also focusing on Ren's helmet, Ranzato comments that Ren wears a "mask simply to emulate his predecessor," thus, the donning of his helmet does not imply, as it did for Darth Vader, a complete transition to the dark side, but rather, a pale imitation.[26] The degree to which Ren fails to personify the shadow has even led to the fan theory that Ren has not turned to the dark side at all, but has committed himself to it in order to bring it down, similar to the role that Severus Snape plays in the *Harry Potter* series.[27]

Other Potential Shadows

A plausible explanation for the failure of Ren's character to provide us with an effective shadow is, of course, that he is not the shadow (or at least not the shadow we are looking for). Another look at Campbell's work reveals a very exciting possibility. Because, according to Jung, the shadow represents the repressed aspects of the hero, it must always be the same gender as the hero.[28] Therefore, because we have a female hero, we might expect a female shadow! *The Force Awakens* and *Bloodline* give us two possibilities for this role.

The first of these is the only woman we see belonging to the First Order, Captain Phasma. The first thing we notice about her, and what distinguishes her from the other stormtroopers under her command, is her armor. It is "coated in salvaged chromium from a Naboo yacht once

24. Matyszczyk, "New Star Wars."
25. Cusmano, "Fan Reactions."
26. Cited in Esteves, "New 'Star Wars.'"
27. Cusmano, "Fan Reactions."
28. Campbell, *Pathways to Bliss*, 75.

owned by Emperor Palpatine. Its polished finish helps reflect harmful radiation, but it serves primarily as a symbol of past power."[29] Donning this symbol of the power of the Emperor may be a foreshadowing of her future prospects for power. Phasma is also not one to shy away from battle, as she insists on participating in all storm trooper missions, and has dedicated herself (perhaps even obsessively) to training her troops and ensuring that "only the best soldiers wear the armor of the First Order." As the Captain of the military force of the First Order, who pays "little heed to outdated notions of inequality between genders, an idea common in undeveloped worlds," Phasma may be someone to watch out for as we continue to seek our shadow.[30]

The other possibility for a female shadow is presented in *Bloodline*, where we learn that it is in fact a woman, Lady Carise Sindian, who is behind the organization of the First Order. Carise's position within the Senate enabled her to search for and organize former Imperial officers into an army, which she was also instrumental in funding. Although the First Order remained largely underground at the time of *Bloodline*, she looks forward to the day the Centrists (her political party, which, contrary to the Populists, Leia's party, favors a more powerful government and military), will break away from the New Republic, strengthened by their First Order army. It is also Carise who discovers the secret of Leia's parentage, and is instrumental in revealing it to the Senate.[31]

Final Reflections

Of course, because we simply have the first of three installments of this new trilogy, Ren could very well turn out to be the shadow he aspires to be, and which the structure of myth requires. However, this seems doubtful, considering just how much emphasis has been placed on his internal struggle against the light. Nevertheless, if Ren is in fact our shadow, analysis needs to go beyond simply addressing his role in the story or audience reactions to him, and must also consider what we are losing if this is the shadow we are confronted with in one of our most important and influential myths. If, as Campbell argues, the purpose of mythology is to help us integrate the

29. Hidalgo, *Star Wars*, 27.

30. Ibid., 27.

31. Gray, *Bloodline*, 226 and 328.

various aspects of ourselves, and therefore make the necessary transitions to live successful lives, we are, it seems to me, in quite a bit of trouble.

And this trouble extends beyond the *Star Wars* universe to other popular culture phenomena, which increasingly present us with heroes and villains that are, at best, ambiguous, and, at worst, indistinguishable. Some important examples of this are found in the realm of superheroes, where we might expect to find our most reliable, or at least identifiable heroes and villains. Instead, we are presented with heroes who fight one another, rather than villains, (*Batman v Superman*; *Captain America: Civil War*), or villains who are sympathetic or even working for the greater good, (Magneto in *X-Men First Class*, or the protagonists in *Suicide Squad*). In contrast to the previous ages of comic books, our present age is characterized by ambiguity and a loss of identifiable shadows and heroes.[32]

When interpreted in light of Campbell's work, the failure of our popular culture myths to provide us with a shadow that can be successfully confronted and integrated has detrimental consequences. It threatens our ability to heed our calls to adventure, navigate the challenges in our lives, and integrate the various repressed aspects of our psyches, especially our shadows. If we are unable to confront and integrate our shadows we are denied the possibility of tapping into our greatest and most important potentials, our universal sources of freedom and power. There is also the possibility that failing to acknowledge and confront our shadows increases our chances of being consumed by them. In other words, we give more power to our darkness by denying it. As we fail to integrate our shadows in an effective way, we also cease to expect others to do so. The ultimate result of these lapses is that we not only lose our villains (which are important in their own right), but we also lose our heroes, as these are, after all, those who have confronted and assimilated their shadows, not only in myth, but in "real life" as well.

Postscript: *The Last Jedi*

Episode VIII does not seem to present us with an alternate villain to Ren. Lady Carise does not appear in the film at all, and though Captain Phasma does have a more dominant role, taking on Finn in a one-on-one duel, she does not confront our hero, Rey, in a significant way. We are therefore left with Ren as the only villain. However, much like in *The Force Awakens*, the

32. Oropeza, "Introduction," 10–18.

theme of abandonment and rejection, rather than anger and attachment, explain his actions in the new film. We learn, for example, that his murder of those training alongside him is motivated by waking up to Luke trying to kill him. This experience exacerbates his feeling of abandonment by his parents, as the only person he felt he could trust has also abandoned—and in fact rejected—him. The theme continues throughout the film, appearing next when Snoke criticizes Ren's weakness and inability to defeat Rey. This rejection from the one he turned to after Luke causes him to smash his helmet, the true symbol of the shadow he tries so hard to embrace. Next, he turns to Rey, but she also rejects him, even after he kills Snoke. This leaves Ren essentially aimless, without any meaningful connections, and seeking only power. When he leads the First Order to the hideout of the Rebel Alliance, he gets another chance to complete his transition to the dark side by killing not only Luke, but also his mother (which he was unable to do earlier in the film). However, because he is not aware of the effect his actions have on Luke (who is of course not actually present), and because he fails to kill the rebels and Leia, his transition is, once again, incomplete.

What all of this amounts to is that Ren has in fact fallen further from Campbell's archetype of the shadow. Rather than confronting and assimilating the dark aspects of his own being, he seeks attachment from both heroes and villains, looking desperately for someone to connect himself to, in order to develop either side of his ambiguous nature. When these attempts fail, he is left alone, but with the power of the First Order behind him. However, because there is no indication that he is in fact invested in their goals and ideology, and because he fails to complete his own transition to the dark side, he remains essentially aimless and un-predictable—and also, perhaps, increasingly dangerous. Although Ren is our villain, he does not provide the opportunity for the confrontation and assimilation of the shadow that Campbell's framework necessitates. The function he does seem to serve, however, is to mirror our contemporary context, where the evil of our real life villains is not the result of principle or conviction, but of reactionary impulsivity attached to nothing but the quest for power. This opens up questions about how myth can help us navigate such a context, if it no longer provides us with extremes to avoid and ideals to strive towards.

Bibliography

Campbell, Joseph. *The Hero with a Thousand Faces*. Princeton, NJ: Princeton University Press, 1968.

———. *Pathways to Bliss: Mythology and Personal Transformation*. Edited by David Kudler. Novato, CA: New World Library, 2004.

"Cave of Evil." *Wookiepedia*. http://starwars.wikia.com/wiki/Cave_of_Evil.

Cusmano, Katherine. "Fan Reactions Prove How Divisive 'Star Wars' Villains Can Be." *Bustle*, December 23, 2015. https://www.bustle.com/articles/131711-fan-reactions-to-kylo-ren-prove-how-divisive-star-wars-villains-can-be.

Esteves, Junno Arocho. "New 'Star Wars' Villains Not Evil Enough, Says Vatican Movie Critic." *Catholic News Service*, December 21, 2015. http://www.catholicnews.com/services/englishnews/2015/new-star-wars-villains-not-evil-enough-says-vatican-movie-critic.cfm.

Flotmann, Christina. *Ambiguity in Star Wars and Harry Potter: A (Post)Structuralist Reading of Two Popular Myths*. Bielefeld, Germany: Transcript, 2013.

Gordon, Andrew. "*Star Wars*: A Myth for Our Time." In *Screening the Sacred: Religion, Myth, and Ideology in Popular American Film*, edited by Joel W. Martin and Conrad E. Ostwalt, 73–82. Boulder, CO: Westview, 1995. Originally published in *Literature/Film Quarterly* 6:4 (Fall 1978) 314–26.

Gray, Claudia. *Bloodline*. New York: Del Rey, 2016.

Hidalgo, Pablo. *Star Wars: The Force Awakens: The Visual Dictionary*. New York: DK Penguin Random House, 2015.

Jung, Carl G. *The Archetypes and the Collective Unconscious*. Translated by R.F.C. Hull. Princeton, NJ: Princeton University Press, 1971.

Last, Shari. *Star Wars: Beware the Sith*. New York: DK, 2012.

Matyszczyk, Chris. "New Star Wars Movie Not Evil Enough, Vatican Paper Says." *cnet*, December 22, 2015. https://www.cnet.com/news/vatican-newspaper-says-star-wars-the-force-awakens-not-evil-enough.

McDowell, John C. *The Gospel According to Star Wars: Faith, Hope, and the Force*. Louisville: Westminster John Knox, 2007.

Oropeza. B. J. "Introduction: Superhero Myth and the Restoration of Paradise." In *The Gospel According to Superheroes: Religion and Popular Culture*, 1–19. New York: Peter Lang, 2006.

Secrets of The Force Awakens: *A Cinematic Journey*. Directed by Laurent Bouzereau. 2016. Disc 2. *Star Wars: The Force Awakens*. Blu-Ray. Burbank: Buena Vista Home Entertainment, 2016.

CHAPTER 3

LEIA "THE HUTT SLAYER" AND REY "THE NEXT GENERATION BADASS BOSS BITCH"

Heroism, Gender, and Fan Appreciation

CHRIS KLASSEN

Abstract: Joseph Campbell enunciates a very specific story of the hero; George Lucas tells that story through the narrative of Luke Skywalker. Like many of the examples Campbell looks to, Lucas's hero is a young male coming of age in a time of turmoil. Many have taken this model of the hero to be an essentially masculine role. Some suggest, however, an alternate model for a feminine hero: the heroine's journey. With the new telling of the myth in *The Force Awakens* it seems there is no need for an alternate model; Rey follows the pattern that Luke did very closely. Looking to Rey as the first female hero of the *Star Wars* world is problematic though, as it ignores the very heroic role of the much earlier character, Leia. However, Leia does not match the pattern Campbell describes. Thus, it behooves us to consider that there are more ways to be a hero than Campbell suggests. Rey is a hero who goes on an individual journey to find power within herself (much as Luke did). Leia, on the other hand, is a hero who holds political leadership and is determined to free her community from the limiting, rigid, and oppressive social structures of the Empire, and later the First Order. While neither role is essentially gendered, the stories of these women speak to a culture that has struggled with gender division and discrimination and make possible what was once unthinkable.

S torytelling is a method of naming the possible. While stories may not be literally true, they can become true through the operationalization of the ideas into real-life scenarios. To be more clear: stories speak truth. This is both a positive and negative element of storytelling. If all the stories we tell say one thing, we believe it to be true. This can be limiting to imagination as well as social and cultural interactions. However, when stories tell of breaches in limiting, rigid, and oppressive social structures, they can lead to emancipation and empowerment. Mythology, in particular, holds this power in a way that has immense impact on cultural values: both the limiting and the empowering varieties. As Joseph Campbell writes, myths "have been the living inspiration of whatever else may have appeared out of the activities of the human body and mind."[1]

The *Star Wars* stories are mythology for the modern ages. At least this was the intent of George Lucas. In an interview with Bill Moyers, Lucas explains that he wanted new generations to engage with the old stories, the old mythologies, but in a new way.[2] The old mythologies that Lucas refers to here are those stories of heroism highlighted by his friend and mentor, Joseph Campbell. Campbell enunciates a very specific story of the hero; Lucas tells that story through the narrative of Luke Skywalker and his discovery of the Force. Like many of the examples Campbell looks to, Lucas' hero is a young male coming of age in a time of turmoil. Many have taken this model of the hero to be an essentially masculine role. Some, as we will see, suggest an alternate model for a feminine hero: the heroine's journey. With the new telling of the myth in *The Force Awakens* it seems there is no need for an alternate model; Rey follows the pattern that Luke did very closely. So, perhaps the hero is not masculine after all. I argue that looking to Rey as the first female hero of the *Star Wars* world is problematic as it ignores the very heroic role of the much earlier character, Leia. However, Leia does not match the pattern Campbell describes. Thus, it behooves us to consider that there are more ways to be a hero than Campbell, and Lucas, suggest. Rey is a specific type of hero that goes on an individual journey to find power within herself (much as Luke did). Leia, on the other hand, is a hero who holds political leadership and is determined to free her community from the limiting, rigid, and oppressive social structures of the Empire, and later the First Order. While neither role is essentially gendered, the stories of

1. Campbell, *The Hero*, 3.
2. Moyers, *The Mythology.*

these women speak to a culture that has struggled with gender division and discrimination and make possible what was once unthinkable.

The Hero

Most discussions of heroism and mythology route back to the work of Joseph Campbell. His well-known structure of the hero's journey, simplified as separation, initiation, and return, can be seen throughout world storytelling. For any discussion of *Star Wars* an appeal to this structure is basic. George Lucas specifically based his story of Luke Skywalker and his initiation into the world of the Force on the hero's journey. Lucas's goal in his storytelling was to tell the old myth in a new format.[3] I think it is safe to say that he succeeded, at least in the original series.

The hero, according to Campbell, is faced with a challenge and needs to leave his home to take on an adventure. Through this adventure, he encounters a mentor and various trials (including often a temptress) and eventually he needs to face death. He overcomes the trials and is granted some prize or ability to take with him to return to his home, as a new man. The masculine language in this description is intentional on my part, though not necessarily essential to Campbell's structure. Campbell does allow that the hero could be "man or woman."[4] So many of his examples, though, are of male heroes that it is easy to see how one could think the hero's journey is a masculine endeavor.

Some have suggested the need to articulate a feminine version of the hero's journey. One such scholar is Valerie Estelle Frankel, who suggests that the heroine's journey is similar to the hero's journey, but has some significant differences as well. She bases her analysis on stories of remarkable women and goddesses from a variety of cultures. The biggest difference between the hero's and heroine's journey is the end goal. The hero (male) acquires a specific prize, whether it be a magical sword or the power of the Jedi. He is on a quest to conquer evil and bring back the prized object or ability for the benefit of his community. In that quest, the hero (male) needs to confront his father to be able to separate himself from that influence and become his own man. A heroine (female) is instead on a quest to become the all-powerful mother. Thus, Frankel titles her book, *From Girl to Goddess*. The heroine (female) finds power within herself, rather than acquiring it in an

3. Moyers, *The Mythology*.
4. Campbell, *The Hero*, 19.

object. And she finds it not through slaying the dragon, but through using her intellect and patience through a long and arduous process, a process that often lacks the glory and spotlight of heroic (male) adventure.

Frankel is motivated to tell the heroine's stories because she sees our society lacking in tales of successful and strong women. There are far too many damsels in distress in the typical heroic adventure. When looking to popular culture we can certainly see an increase in female heroic roles in the past few years. However, Frankel has concerns there as well. She does not want women limited to the hero (male) role because she sees it as inherently masculine. Frankel writes:

> In today's society, women oppressed by hero myths see only two choices: Be the helpless princess sobbing for rescue, or be the knight, helmeted and closed off in a cubicle of steel, armored against the natural world, featureless behind a helmet. Only men or those who act like them, with business suits and power lunches and strategy charts, will succeed.[5]

Men and women should have different stories, according to Frankel. Thus, there is a strict differentiation between the hero and the heroine.

Frankel and Campbell are both Jungians and as such frame their understanding of these mythic structures as archetypes. For full disclosure, I must admit that I am not a Jungian. I distrust the rhetoric of archetypes for its simplistic universalizing of complex cultural systems. I also do not understand masculinity and femininity to be clear categories that inhere in our bodies. Sex and gender are much more fluid and complicated than Jung allowed for. Nevertheless, I am intrigued by the two stories laid out in the hero's and heroine's journeys. Could the juxtaposition of these two stories help to highlight that there are multiple ways to be heroic?

In 1983 Carol Gilligan published a study of the development of moral maturity based on her response to the theories of her teacher, Lawrence Kohlberg. Kohlberg believed that moral maturity was characterized by adopting abstract universal ethical principles. Unsurprisingly, Kohlberg came to his conclusions based on his studies with boys. When he then studied girls and their moral development he found that they typically did not reach the same height of moral maturity as boys. They had trouble with the abstract universal ethics based on individualism and rights.[6] Gilligan's study showed that often girls developed a different kind of ethics, not a less

5. Frankel, *From Girl to Goddess*, 3.
6. Kohlberg, "The Development."

developed one. Girls were more likely to develop what Gilligan calls an ethic of care that focuses on community well-being and interaction rather than the ethic of justice characterized by the more individualistic abstract universals. However, Gilligan does not conclude that girls have one ethic and boys another. Rather, she suggests that there are these two ethics and based on cultural stereotypes and expectations, boys are more likely to develop an ethic of justice and girls are more likely to develop an ethic of care. But either ethic can be embraced by any gender. The ethics themselves are not inherently gendered, just the cultural context.[7]

Perhaps the types of heroic narratives should be thought of in a similar way. The individualistic hero questing for glory and a great prize to bring back to the community is one kind of hero. The thoughtful and patient hero developing into a leader for the ultimate benefit of the community is another kind of hero. Sure, we may have more male individualistic questing heroes in our popular culture and more female heroes building family and community, but that is cultural context and expectation of gendered roles. And these gendered roles are changing in many Western cultural contexts.

Star Wars has always had a female hero; she was just not a fit for Campbell's hero's journey. However, now with *The Force Awakens* we have both. The rest of this essay will examine how Rey and Leia are both heroes, but in very different ways. I will outline their stories in light of the two journeys provided by Campbell and Frankel. But ultimately the heroism of these characters is judged by the viewers. I draw on audience reactions to these characters to flesh out the meaning and importance of these heroic women.

I need to make a note about language. In my discussion of Campbell and Frankel, I have been clarifying hero (male) and heroine (female). The use of "hero" and "heroine" reinforces the differentness between men and women in a way that reifies a rigid dualistic gendered differentiation. The term "heroine" is a diminutive term designed to mark women off from the norm. I will use the term "hero" from now on to refer to a hero of any gender.

---

7. Gilligan, *In a Different Voice.*

Rey: "a fighter and a survivor and a nurturer and an all-around badass"[8]

If Luke Skywalker is a clear model of Campbell's hero, then so is Rey. Her story, so far, is much the same as Luke's. She is living on a desert planet when her life is disrupted by the arrival of a droid from another world. Luke was living on a desert planet when his life was disrupted by the arrival of droids from another world. Rey is given a task to complete: return the droid to the Resistance. Luke was given a task to complete: help Obi-Wan return the droids to the Rebel Alliance. Rey encounters trials and barriers but eventually finds a mentor in Han Solo and a guide in Maz Kanata. Luke encountered trials and barriers but finds a mentor in Obi-Wan and a guide in Yoda. Both must face their own fears and commit to the journey. Rey witnesses the death of her mentor and faces the power of the evil First Order. Luke witnessed the death of his mentor and faces the power of the evil Empire. Rey visits a distant planet to receive training from a reluctant Jedi Master, and subsequently leaves before her training is complete to face Kylo Ren. Luke visits a distant plant to receive training from a reluctant Jedi Master, and subsequently leaves before his training is complete to face Darth Vader. The parallels are glaringly obvious.

In some ways Rey could be seen as an improved Luke. After all, while she is naïve and young, she is less annoyingly trite than Luke was on Tatooine. It is hard to imagine Rey whining about wanting to go pick up some power converters. She certainly seems more skilled than Luke was, but then in her story she has no family to support and love her, while Luke does. She starts off with greater resilience. Luke needs to learn to be resilient.

Some critics have argued that Rey is too much improved. Screenwriter Max Landis suggests that *The Force Awakens* is a "fanfic movie with a Mary Sue as the main character."[9] But what is a Mary Sue? The title of Mary Sue comes from the world of sci-fi fan fiction, stories written by fans about their favorite characters or sci-fi worlds. A Mary Sue is a character that is created, typically by a female fan writer, who is perfect in every way. She is stronger and faster and smarter than any of the male characters. She is often a stand- in for the writer herself, who fantasizes about living in the sci-fi world. Mary Sue was the character of one of these stories written by a *Star Trek* fan; the name became synonymous with the trope. What does

8. Garber, "*Star Wars.*"
9. Quoted in Kain, "No, Rey."

it mean, though, to call Rey a Mary Sue? Eric Kain makes a good argument for Rey not being perfect: she can fly the Millennium Falcon, but is clumsy at first; she picks up on the Jedi mind trick fairly quickly, but only after Kylo Ren has been in her head (and possibly introducing some of his knowledge to her); she seems to defeat Kylo Ren fairly easily in the final battle, but he has already been injured and is not at his best.[10] So, why the accusation? While Kain does not come right out and say it, Megan Crouse does: "calling Rey a Mary Sue more often just serves to shut her out of the same hero-space in which Luke and Anakin Skywalker reside."[11] She seems too good, for a woman.

What makes Rey stand out for many viewers is the very fact that she is a woman in a heroic role that has previously been reserved for men. True, we have seen an increase in women taking these roles in popular culture: Ripley in the *Alien* franchise, Merida in *Brave*, and Katniss in *The Hunger Games*, as examples. But Rey is the first in the *Star Wars* world, followed closely by Jyn in *Rogue One*. What does it mean for fans to have a woman in this role?

For some it is a reinforcement of their knowledge that they can be heroes too. Many fans commenting online are long-time *Star Wars* viewers. They remember, as Syreeta McFadden does, playing Luke as children.[12] They didn't allow gender to get in their way then, but having a woman in the role does validate their experiences. Rey fills a gap that their younger selves "desperately needed as a child," says Sarah Galo.[13] But it is more than just having a woman in a hero role. It is also the way Rey takes on that role. McFadden writes, "Rey isn't someone's romantic interest, she's a warrior."[14] Megan Garber concurs: "No distressing damsel, she's instead a fighter and a survivor and a nurturer and an all-around badass."[15] Ben Child adds, "it's abundantly obvious that our new hero is more than capable of matching the men for combat skills."[16] Rey is a warrior with skills and determination. She is not a watered-down version of a hero. As Rebecca Carroll proclaims,

10. Quoted in Kain, "No, Rey."

11. Crouse, "*Star Wars.*"

12. Syreeta McFadden in Karvelas et al., "*Star Wars.*"

13. Karvelas et al., "*Star Wars.*"

14. Ibid.

15. Garber, "*Star Wars.*"

16. Child, "Is *Star Wars.*"

Rey is "a next generation badass boss bitch that we and Princess Leia can be proud of."[17]

Rey the warrior.

The story of Rey is one of an individual coming to know herself and learn of her own inner power. For Rey, this power is not only the Force, but the will and determination to move towards a goal and help the people around her. She shows courage and strength of will, traits commonly associated with the hero. Furthermore, she is read by her fans as a symbol of personal power for women. She does not need male help, as is evident in her questioning why Finn keeps taking her hand. Yet she does need help (not defined as male). She knows her skills and will use them. But she also will draw on the community around her as long as it will take her where she needs to go. Rey as hero provides a personal role model in a context of individualism and standing up for one's self. Be clear, this is not a selfish individualism, but an individualism that promises the work of one person can change the world. Rey is the hero changing the world, and in so doing, she encourages women and girls that they too can be that hero. Perhaps, like McFadden who played Luke as a child, men and boys will be encouraged by Rey as well.

17. Syreeta McFadden in Karvelas et al., "Star Wars."

Leia: "a player in a high-stakes political game"[18]

While Rey may be the first female hero of the individualistic sort in the *Star Wars* filmic world, she is not the first female hero. Right at the beginning we have Princess Leia. However, Princess Leia does not follow the structure laid out in Campbell's hero's journey. In fact she has no real journey at all. She is already there.

Leia is a woman of power. Though we first meet her as a young woman, she already has a political position both on her home planet of Alderaan and in the Rebel Alliance. She is heroic in her leadership position and her determination to work within a group for the betterment of all the peoples of the galaxy. In many ways, Leia, even at her young age, takes on the role Frankel discusses in her rendition of the heroine's journey. She has become the great Mother, but this is not a figure of pure nurturing and love. Like the Great Goddesses Frankel draws upon, Leia is fiercely protective and willing to fight for and with her people.

Leia is remembered by many viewers as a female warrior in a world with very few females of any kind. In fact, Darren Franich, in an *Entertainment Weekly* article, argues that "she is the fiercest soldier of the main cast of characters."[19] Our first full view of her face-forward involves her pulling out a blaster and shooting storm troopers. When Luke and Han supposedly rescue her, she is the one who grabs Luke's blaster and takes charge, getting them out of the hopeless situation the men have created. She runs through the Death Star shooting storm troopers with little concern for her own safety and holds her own in any combat scene. She shows that, yes, girls can fight.

But she doesn't just fight. She takes charge. During their escape in *Star Wars: A New Hope*, Leia proclaims to Han Solo: "I don't know who you are, or where you come from, but from now on you take orders from me." This is not just royal pretension on her part. She knows the context, she understands the stakes, and she will do what it takes to succeed in her mission. Cher Martinetti argues, "It's one of the first times there's been a woman in a leadership position in fiction who wasn't reduced to the stereotype of being too emotional to effectively do her job."[20] This is the whole point of Leia's heroism. She is a woman in a leadership position. She is involved in politics.

18. Bell, "Princess Leia."
19. Franich, "How Carrie Fisher."
20. Martinetti, "Why Princess Leia."

She can take charge at an administrative level and is fully invested in the institutional power structure.

Leia's institutional authority is in full view at the end of Episode IV, as she hands out medals to Luke and Han.

It is hard to talk of Leia as a feminist role model for girls and women without addressing the problem of the gold bikini. I would like to quote, at some length, fan Emily L. Houser's response to this scene:

> Mention the character of Princess Leia to the average resident of Planet Earth and two images come to mind: White-robed Leia with her double-Cinnabon hairdo, and golden-bikinied "Slave Leia."
>
> This despite the fact that she's in that bikini for less than three of the 399 minutes that make up the original *Star Wars* trilogy (yes, I did the math); despite the fact that it was forced on her as humiliation and punishment after being caught infiltrating Jabba the Hutt's lair disguised as a bounty hunter and carrying a thermo-detonator (aka: space grenade) in order to rescue Han Solo (again, might I add—to rescue Han Solo *again*); and despite the fact that as her final act in Jabba's clutches, she kills the universe's greatest crime lord *with the very chain he used to bind her.*
>
> But sure, yeah: "Slave Leia."
>
> This is, after all, what we do to women every day—we reduce them to their weakest, meekest, most domesticated iterations. If women are allowed to be sexual, they must be sexual in a way that meets heterosexual male expectations . . . Stop already with the "Slave Leia" crap. That woman in the gold bikini? That's Leia the Hutt Slayer. So she is, and so shall she be named.[21]

21. Hauser, "Princess Leia."

Houser's renaming of Leia as "the Hutt Slayer" is indicative of the way many women, particularly women growing up in the 1970s and 1980s, have adopted Leia as hero, even if she does not play out the hero's journey. Getting caught up in the instances where Leia is captured and demeaned ignores the considerably more common accounts of her leadership. She is not, at any point, a damsel in distress. At least, not any more than Han Solo is a damsel in distress when he is captured. Leia is, as blogger Morgan Leigh Bell argues, "a player in a high stakes political game."[22]

Not only is Leia never a damsel in distress, she is also not defined by her romantic side-story. The witty banter between Leia and Han emphasizes their equality and provides comic relief, but never gets in the way of Leia's mission. Cher Martinetti highlights the importance of this element of Leia's character for girls and women:

> We need to see women who put their careers first, and if and when they fall in love, don't lose themselves in that relationship. We need to see women characters who can be powerful leaders and equally powerful soldiers. And most of all we need female characters that never allow anyone to control their narrative, that continue to defy sexist and ignorant tropes. After all, these fictional characters that little girls look up to may one day shape the type of women they are determined to be.[23]

The sentiment expressed by Martinetti here is perhaps the strongest reason for little fan discussion of Padmé Amidala as a feminist role model. While in *The Phantom Menace* she shows potential to be the kind of heroic leader that Leia is, the story turn in the next two films completely substitutes her agency for her romance. She loses importance in the story as anything other than Anakin's love interest.

Leia's leadership role is emphasized even more in *The Force Awakens* where Leia is now General Organa. A Princess may be born into her position of authority; a general earns it. As with her roles in the earlier films, Leia takes charge. Her fluctuating relationship with Han still does not get in the way of her leadership role, and she is now actually a mother. Fan Laurie Penny comments on this aspect: "Carrie Fisher has given us the thing even the most far-flung space fantasist has struggled to imagine— a middle-aged mother who is just as powerful and important as she was as a nubile princess. General Leia does my feminist fangirl heart a lot of

22. Bell, "Princess Leia."
23. Martinetti, "Why Princess Leia."

good."[24] This is certainly a story that has rarely been told in popular culture, though Frankel does highlight older mythological versions in her book. But Leia is not just a mother; she is a mother mourning the loss of her child. This is important because it gives us the story of the heroic leader who can still care, grieve, and love. She is not immune to the realities of living. But she does not let them stop her from doing her job, fighting for justice, and protecting those she loves.

Conclusion

Leia and Rey are important heroes in the *Star Wars* world. This is a world in which there is a continual battle between good and evil. Though much of the internal mythology is about balance within the Force, that balance seems to require the good guys to win. The evil forces are clearly evil, fascist, and totalitarian. The heroes are fighting for democracy, equality, and freedom. The original films were obviously drawing on Cold War imagery; the leaders in the Empire always struck me as Soviet in appearance. In *The Force Awakens* the visuals around the First Order point to the Nazis. In either case, the fight for democracy, equality, and freedom is a heroic fight. Both the individuals on the front lines and the leaders of the Rebellion/Resistance are portrayed in heroic ways. Having male and female warriors and leaders tells us the story that men and women can equally engage in this heroism. This does not make the heroic roles either masculine or feminine. Men and women do not necessarily do these roles differently. It is the roles, themselves, that are different. Sometimes someone needs to take the risks to stand up to the enemy face-to-face. In *The Last Jedi*, both Rey and Luke exemplify this. However, sometimes one needs to look less like a typical hero and be a leader. This may include retreating to protect the community so it can live to continue the fight. Leia and her protégé, Vice-Admiral Amilyn Holdo, take this position. However, in the end, so does the 'reckless flyboy' Poe Dameron. Gender is not really the defining element of these heroic roles. But if you have always heard the story told about the warrior or the leader as "he," hearing it told as a "she" can be profoundly disruptive and empowering. The story speaks a truth; it makes something possible in the cultural imagination.

24. Laurie Penny in Karvelas et al., "*Star Wars*."

New fans and new heroes: twin sisters Jessie and Jamie as Jyn and Rey for Hallowe'en 2017 in Toronto. Photo courtesy of Lisa Gerlsbeck.

Bibliography

Bell, Morgan Leigh. "Princess Leia: Hero or Damsel in Distress." *Opus* (2004). https://sites.google.com/site/morganleighbell/princessleia-heroordamselindistress.

Campbell, Joseph. *The Hero with a Thousand Faces.* Princeton, NJ: Princeton University Press, 1949.

Child, Ben. "Is *Star Wars: The Force Awakens* Really Female-Friendly?" *The Guardian*, December 16, 2015. https://www.theguardian.com/film/2015/dec/16/star-wars-the-force-awakens-jj-abrams-bechdel-test-female-friendly.

Crouse, Megan. "*Star Wars*: Analyzing the Female Characters of *The Force Awakens.*" *Den of Geek*, July 16, 2016. http://www.denofgeek.com/us/movies/star-wars/251331/star-wars-analyzing-the-female-characters-of-the-force-awakens.

Franich, Darren. "How Carrie Fisher Created Princess Leia and Reclaimed Her Legacy." *Entertainment Weekly*, December 27, 2016. http://ew.com/movies/2016/12/27/carrie-fisher-princess-leia-legacy.

Frankel, Valerie Estelle. *From Girl to Goddess: The Heroine's Journey through Myth and Legend.* Jefferson, NC: McFarland, 2010.

Garber, Megan. "*Star Wars*: The Feminism Awakens." *The Atlantic*, December 19, 2015. http://www.theatlantic.com/entertainment/archive/2015/12/star-wars-the-feminism-awakens/420843.

Gilligan, Carol. *In a Different Voice: Psychological Theory and Women's Development.* Cambridge, MA: Harvard University Press, 1983.

Hauser, Emily L. "Princess Leia, Feminist Hero." *The Week*, December 16, 2015. http://theweek.com/articles/594202/princess-leia-feminist-hero.

Kain, Erik. "No, Rey from *Star Wars: The Force Awakens* Is Not a Mary Sue." *Forbes*, January 4, 2016. http://web.archive.org/web/20161207100745/http://www.forbes.com/sites/erikkain/2016/01/04/no-rey-from-star-wars-the-force-awakens-is-not-a-mary-sue/#637f4eb3f12b.

Karvelas, Patricia et al. "*Star Wars* Is a Game-Changer, Awakening the Feminist Force in Little Girls Everywhere." *The Guardian*, December 30, 2015. https://www.theguardian.com/commentisfree/2015/dec/30/star-wars-is-a-game-changer-awakening-the-feminist-force-in-little-girls-everywhere.

Kohlberg, Lawrence. "The Development of Modes of Thinking and Choices in Years 10 to 16." PhD diss., University of Chicago, 1958.

Martinetti, Cher. "Why Princess Leia Is My Hero, and the One All Girls Deserve." *SyfyWire*, May 4, 2015. http://www.blastr.com/2015-5-4/star-wars-day-why-princess-leia-my-hero-and-one-all-girls-deserve.

Moyers, Bill. *The Mythology of Star Wars with George Lucas and Bill Moyers*. Films for the Humanities and Sciences, 1999. https://vimeo.com/groups/183185/videos/38026023.

CHAPTER 4

I'VE HEARD THIS SOMEWHERE BEFORE

The Myth-Making Implications of Han and Leia's Theme

KUTTER CALLAWAY

Abstract: This chapter explores the role that music plays in the fan reception of *The Force Awakens* by considering the ways in which the film's music connects it to the larger mythological landscape of the *Star Wars* universe. By focusing on one of the series' more prominent musical figures (the "Han and Leia" theme), we can see that fans are responding not only to narrative developments in Episode VII, but also to the unique, myth-making capacity of music. More specifically, as it concerns the franchise's identity politics and its historically fraught conceptions of gender, we can speculate as to whether this music can be understood as signaling a progressive move within the *Star Wars* mythology or if it is, rather, a mere recapitulation of the status quo.

the risk of understatement, describing fan culture is a complicated business. But when it comes to *Star Wars*—a franchise that is now permanently ensconced in the contemporary cultural imagination—this complexity shifts into an entirely different register. Take, for example, the variety of conflicting fan responses to a single scene from *Star Wars: The Force Awakens*. In one of Kylo Ren's many dark side-induced outbursts of violence (*spoiler alert*), he murders his own father, Han Solo. Rey and Chewbacca, first-hand witnesses to the killing of their beloved friend, flee the exploding Starkiller Base and return to the site where the Resistance

61

fighters have gathered. As the Wookiee and his preternaturally gifted female friend disembark from the Millennium Falcon, the first person they see is General Leia Organa, mother to the patricidal Kylo Ren. Instantly, Leia's and Rey's eyes meet. The camera cuts between medium close-up shots of both characters as they move slowly but steadfastly toward one another. While the rest of the Resistance gathers off camera, these two women—one a high-ranking general and the other an unknown orphan—embrace.

As sound effects drop entirely from the soundtrack and music moves to the foreground, Leia and Rey share in each other's grief, even if only for a moment. They have never met before (as far as the audience knows), but neither utters a word. Nor do they need to. Even though the narrative has provided virtually no information up to this point about their relationship, "the music seems to intuit connections that are beyond immediate rational comprehension."[1]

1. Buhler, "Star Wars," 44. Buhler is speaking here of the first time the Force theme is heard in A New Hope, but as will become evident, according to my reading of The Force

To put it mildly, this sequence managed to generate various levels of outrage among *Star Wars* aficionados. According to a number of the more passionate fans of the film, it was simply unthinkable that Leia would fail to acknowledge Chewbacca, Solo's lifelong friend who passes somewhat conspicuously through the scene (see screenshots above).[2] Wouldn't Han's faithful companion be the one in need of consolation, deserving of at least as much comfort as the young girl who hardly knew the infamous smuggler? Chewbacca may have a tough-as-nails image to maintain, but he's no monster. After all, Wookiees have feelings too. At the very least, he deserves better than to be snubbed by Leia, who is not only his longtime friend but also the leading figure of the Resistance.

To his credit, writer and director J. J. Abrams responded directly to the concerns voiced by the fan base. He admitted that the hug between Leia and Rey (aka "Hug-gate") was a directorial mistake, exacerbated by the fact that Chewbacca was in the scene. Abrams suggested that, if he had simply removed the lumbering Wookiee from the shot, fans would have had no issue with the hug. "But because he was right there, passed by Leia, it felt almost like a slight, which was definitely not the intention."[3] He went on to explain his "mistake" in more detail:

> My thinking at the time was that Chewbacca, despite the pain he was feeling, was focused on trying to save Finn and getting him taken care of. So I tried to have Chewbacca go off with him and focus on Rey, and then have Rey find Leia and Leia find Rey. The idea being that both of them being strong with the Force and never having met, would know about each other—that Leia would have been told about her beyond what we saw onscreen and Rey of course would have learned about Leia. And that reunion would be a meeting and a reunion all in one, and a sort of commiseration of their mutual loss.[4]

But let's be honest: J. J. Abrams can't be trusted, especially when it comes to his films. He's an unreliable narrator, and intentionally so. As others have pointed out, his penchant for misdirection is an integral element of

Awakens, the music functions in a similar capacity in this scene as well.

2. "The controversial hug in 'Star Wars: The Force Awakens' between Leia and Rey created significant buzz because nitpickers felt the general snubbed her long-time friend Chewbacca" (Chiusano, "J. J. Abrams").

3. Sciretta, "Exclusive."

4. Sciretta, "Exclusive."

the larger "Abrams" brand, which hinges upon a dynamic and participatory relationship with fans.[5] Whether it's the television series *Lost*, *Super 8*, the *Star Trek* reboots, or now, with *The Force Awakens*, Abrams is constantly involved in a game of cat and mouse with fans. His films almost always feature a number of narrative "mysteries" and cinematic sleights of hand, which invite audiences to drill beneath the surface in an effort to discover hidden clues that might explain the inexplicable—a form of participatory media consumption known as "forensic fandom."[6] But beyond these formal conventions, which generate their fair share of unexpected reveals and surprising plot twists, Abrams also has a tendency to throw fans off the scent by simply deceiving them.[7] So we have very little reason to accept his claims about the Leia-Rey hug at face value. After all, nothing accidental ends up in the final cut of a film, especially one directed by J. J. Abrams.

Yet, if Abrams-as-auteur is not to be trusted, then what exactly can we make of this scene, both in its own right and as a microcosm of the film's overall reception? And how does it relate to the myth-making dimensions of *The Force Awakens* as one piece of the larger *Star Wars* saga? Again, it's complicated. But I want to suggest in what follows that no critical analysis can do justice to the complex relationship between *Star Wars*

5. Henry Jenkins offers an insightful analysis of the relationship Abrams has developed with his fans. For Jenkins, Abrams's TV and film work serves as a prime example of the upending of the hierarchy between media producers and media consumers—a key turn in what Jenkins now refers to as "participatory culture." It's a form of storytelling that "balances puzzles . . . with backstory . . . and narrative enigmas" (*Convergence Culture*, 122).

6. "[T]hese programs convert many viewers into amateur narratologists, noting patterns and violations of convention, chronicling chronologies, and highlighting both inconsistencies and continuities across episodes and even series—I call this model of engagement '*forensic fandom*.'" (Mittell, *Complex TV*, 52 [emphasis in original].)

7. A prominent example has to do with Abrams denying for months that Benedict Cumberbatch would be playing the character Khan in *Star Trek Into Darkness*. Reflecting on his deception during an interview with MTV, Abrams not only identifies his primary motivation for lying (i.e., to increase the "fun" generated by the mystery), but also acknowledges that his strategy sometimes backfires: "The truth is I think it probably would have been smarter just to say upfront 'This is who [Cumberbatch] is.' It was only trying to preserve the fun of it, and it might have given more time to acclimate and accept that's what the thing was. The truth is because it was so important to the studio that we not angle this thing for existing fans. If we said it was Khan, it would feel like you've really got to know what *Star Trek* is about to see this movie. That would have been limiting. I can understand their argument to try to keep that quiet, but I do wonder if it would have seemed a little bit less like an attempt at deception if we had just come out with it" (Bricken, "J. J. Abrams").

films, filmmakers, and fans without an awareness of how music functions in the series.

Music as Myth-Making: John Williams and Richard Wagner

Truth be told, there simply is no *Star Wars* without the John Williams score. There is no Darth Vader without the "Imperial March," and no Princess Leia without "Princess Leia's Theme." In fact, in the absence of certain pieces of music (e.g., "The Force Theme"), it becomes difficult to speak of any Force at all. As Jim Buhler (along with a whole host of other musicologists) has noted, "from its very first appearance, music is thus linked with the production of myth in *Star Wars*. . . . Indeed, the filmic representation of the Force depends crucially on music."[8]

This is hardly a controversial claim. In terms of the films' reception, the music of *Star Wars* is so fully bound up with its mythic landscape that to talk about the score as if it were a wholly independent entity is to run the risk of drawing analytic distinctions where in fact viewers encounter an integrated whole. Nevertheless, given that our principal concern has to do with how audiences responded to *The Force Awakens*, it is important to call out the unique ways in which music functions in the *Star Wars* saga. And this is because, moreso than any other filmic element, music exists "for" the audience, especially non-diegetic music.[9] In addition, when it comes to the relationship between film-going and myth-making, the music associated with the narrative universe of *Star Wars* is particularly significant because Williams's scores draw quite intentionally upon the myth-making possibilities of the leitmotif—a musical convention that has its roots in the dramas of Richard Wagner.

Of course, to say that a film score is structured by its use of the leitmotif is not to say that it is functioning exactly like the music in a Wagnerian drama. Indeed, in their *Composing for the Films*, Theodor Adorno and Hans Eisler offer a critique of Hollywood's appropriation of the leitmotif,

8. Buhler, "Star Wars," 37, 39.

9. "Non-diegetic" music is music that underscores the diegetic world (i.e., the enclosed narrative world of the characters) but does not have its source within that world. It serves as a buffer between the narrative and the audience, existing in a symbolic realm most often occupied by the implied narrator. As such, this kind of music is principally "for" the audience, offering viewers a particular "take" on the unfolding events within the narrative world. For more on this concept and its implications for theology and religious studies, see Callaway, *Scoring Transcendence*.

noting how film composers often fail to account for the formal requirements of the Wagnerian leitmotif, which needs a much larger canvas if it is
to be anything more than a banal and redundant signpost.[10] In other words,
"The primary purpose of Wagner's leitmotif is the production of myth not
signification. Film music, by contrast, has secularized the leitmotif, demythologizing it precisely by emphasizing its linguistic quality, the process of
signification."[11]

Generally speaking, then, cinematic leitmotifs represent not only an
undoing of Wagner's mythical impulse but also a demythification of the
leitmotif itself. Rather than imbue "dramatic events with metaphysical
significance"[12] as in Wagner's dramas, filmmakers call upon these highly
recognizable musical phrases to do little more than "announce heroes and
situations so as to help the audience to orient itself more easily."[13] For instance, a film's love theme is often inextricably tethered to the two lovers
in a narrative, signaling to the audience that their relationship is either
newly forming, under threat, or painfully absent (or perhaps even all at
once). Likewise, as viewers see the silhouette of a femme fatale, it is highly
likely that they also hear a sultry saxophone playing her melody. And as
the underdog sports team finally vanquishes its bigger and stronger foe,
a reprise of the film's primary leitmotif typically moves to the foreground.
The point in identifying some of these well-worn conventions is that, in
terms of communicating important narrative information to the audience,
filmmakers and composers often leverage the linguistic capacity of music as their preferred means for generating narrative clarity both quickly
and efficiently. In other words, it is to treat music as language—as mere
communication.

Nevertheless, music is still music, which means that it always resists
this kind of semiotic reduction:

> The leitmotif draws attention to itself; it must be heard to perform
> the semiotic function attributed to it. The leitmotif says: listen to
> me, for I am telling you something significant. So long as music
> remains music, however, its meaning remains veiled. . . . Through

---

10. Adorno and Eisler, *Composing*.

11. Buhler, "*Star Wars*," 42. My description of the relationship between Williams,
Wagner, and the music in *Star Wars* is greatly indebted to the work of James Buhler, both
his published work and our personal correspondence.

12 Adorno and Eisler, *Composing*, 5.

13. Adorno, *In Search*, 125. As quoted in Buhler, "*Star Wars*," 43.

the leitmotif, film becomes a mythic discourse, in which its mythic impulse hides behind an apparent demythologization. Demythologization in film music thus comes to serve the function of a more insidious mystification, because that mystification sublates its myth into entertainment, which seeks the status of art while absolving itself of the responsibility that art demands.[14]

To be sure, Williams deploys leitmotifs for semiotic purposes at times. But more than perhaps any other modern film composer, Williams is writing self-consciously mythic music for what is clearly a self-consciously mythic film franchise. And he demonstrates his indebtedness to a Wagnerian model (i.e., music as myth producing) by calling upon music in the various *Star Wars* films as a means for signifying something that lies beyond or outside signification, namely, the Force. But in doing so, Williams faces the same mytho-musical dilemma as Wagner. That is, the various articulations of the key leitmotifs in the *Star Wars* saga are not so much developments of the score's thematic material, but rather, recapitulations. Thus, to quote Buhler again, "nothing actually happens musically in any of these scores. The themes simply remain the same; none of them are really born of a thematic process, despite the obvious motivic relations among the themes. The musical logic throughout *Star Wars* remains that of an original and its derivatives."[15] Or, to put it differently, rather than a progressive movement signaled by a substantive development of the film's primary leitmotifs, the music in *Star Wars* signals a perpetual return to its mythological origin.

A Gendered Origin Myth?

But what, one might ask, does any of this have to do with two women hugging at the end of *The Force Awakens*? Furthermore, how does it shed light on the ways in which fans responded to this particular scene—a response that had at least something to do with Leia choosing to embrace a young woman instead of a hairy, overgrown male? To answer these questions, we first have to acknowledge that, just as *The Force Awakens* has inherited a distinct musical history, so too has it inherited a history fraught by identity politics. But as John Lyden points out in his contribution to this volume, it remains unclear whether *Star Wars* has a particular political point to make and, even if it does, what that point might actually be. Like any sacred text,

14. Buhler, "*Star Wars*," 43–44.

15. Ibid., 53.

myths are opaque entities that resist closure and fixed interpretations. As a result, it seems to be the case that, more often than not, "the political sensibilities of the viewers color what they see in the myth, which was as true of the original films as it is of the newer additions to the canon."[16]

For instance, some critics have gone so far as to suggest that "in the film *Star Wars* . . . the characters Luke Skywalker, Han Solo and Princess Lea enact a patriarchal, bourgeois (liberal humanist), white supremacist narrative in a setting uncannily similar to today's USA."[17] Others have struck an equally critical, but somewhat more charitable note:

> [T]he cinematic product of Lucas' imagination, whether intentionally or not, reflects deep hegemonic currents in the modern American culture by defining women in the narratives from the male perspective. In many ways, this reading should hardly be surprising given the prevalence of the perception of the SW saga as a politically conservative set of texts.[18]

Still others offer a reading of *Star Wars* that moves in both conservative and progressive directions at the same time. For instance, Jeanne Cavelos suggests that, on the one hand, "George Lucas blazed a trail with Leia that many writers have followed, and all viewers who like seeing independent, self-reliant female characters owe him a debt of gratitude." On the other hand, "Leia initially appears to be a powerful figure, a princess and senator and the bearer of key Rebel intelligence. Over the course of the trilogy, though, her importance dwindles and her power evaporates before our eyes."[19]

This diversity of views within the critical scholarship suggests that, when it comes to representations of gender, nothing in the *Star Wars* universe is as straightforward as it might appear at first. Complicating matters further are the number of fans who seem more than willing to "read against the grain" of the culturally encoded identity politics that critics have identified. As Will Brooker notes in *Using the Force: Creativity, Community, and Star Wars Fans*, "[w]omen and girls are into *Star Wars*. Online, female-run communities attract thousands of hits per week. The webmistresses of sites like *Star Wars Chicks* have loved the saga since they were young and found ways to explore it in make-believe games and fiction during their childhood, despite pressure to ditch *Star Wars* and conform to more traditional

16. Lyden, "The More Things Change," 23.

17. Cranny-Francis, "Feminist Futures," 223.

18. McDowell, *Identity Politics*, 79.

19. Cavelos, "Stop Her."

gender roles."[20] A strikingly similar sentiment can be found in the work of feminist scholar Diana Dominguez, who reflects on her original encounter with the *Star Wars* saga as a young girl growing up in the midst of the blossoming feminist movement:

> [I]n May of 1977, finally, I saw, larger than life on the screen, the woman I wanted to become. Here was a woman who could play *like* and *with* the boys, but who didn't have to *become* one of the boys and who could, if and when she wanted to, show she *liked* the boys, a woman who is outspoken, unashamed, and, most importantly, unpunished for being so. . . . Leia is a *hero* without losing her gendered status; she does not have to play the cute, helpless sex kitten or become sexless and androgynous to get what she wants. She can be strong, sassy, outspoken, bossy, and bitchy, and still be respected and seen as feminine.[21]

In no way do any of these viewer accounts deny the reality that "there remains a significant issue to be asked concerning Lucas' space opera over the gendering alterity so that women become alienated, made alien, and thereby disempowered."[22] That being said, though, given the diversity of these on-the-ground responses, the *Star Wars* mythology—as a mythic text—does seem to allow room for a more progressive read of its gender dynamics. In some cases, it even demands it. In fact, in spite of all the drama surrounding Anakin Skywalker, his son Luke, and his grandson Ben, it is becoming increasingly true that, as the *Star Wars* saga unfolds with each subsequent installment, the story is less about the males that comprise the Skywalker lineage and far more about Padmé Amidala, her daughter Leia, and this mysterious yet highly Force-sensitive orphan known simply as Rey. In other words, it may very well be that female fans like the young Diana Dominguez and the modern day Star Wars Chicks have intuited something about the franchise that has always been the case, but is only now being fully realized (*spoiler alert*): *Star Wars* is all about women. And it always has been.

---

20. Brooker, *Using the Force*, 200.

21. Dominguez, "Feminism and the Force," 115–16 [emphasis in original].

22. Cranny-Francis, "Feminist Futures," 223.

Negating the Negation

We can now return full circle to Leia and Rey's hug and why it is so important for us to pay attention to the music we hear when these two women embrace. The leitmotif that underscores the "hug-gate" scene is a slight variation of the musical figure that appears in some form or another throughout the series, most notably as Han Solo and Princess Leia first kiss while on board the Millennium Falcon in *The Empire Strikes Back*. The track itself is titled "Han and Leia" because it is the principal musical figure that signifies their ongoing romance in both episodes V and VI. In *Episode VII: The Force Awakens*, the music seems initially to be following this same pattern of signification, appearing on cue when Han and Leia see one another for the first time. But everything changes when Leia and Rey meet. In this moment, the presence of the leitmotif creates what we might call "a disturbance in the Force." It becomes unmoored from its original pairing (i.e., the Leia/Han romance) and associates itself with an entirely new referent (the mysterious bond between Leia and Rey). In doing so, it not only opens up a number of interpretive possibilities regarding the narrative trajectory of the series, but also retroactively modifies our understanding of all its previous articulations.

In the first and perhaps most obvious sense, the leitmotif that plays during the Leia-Rey hug functions in a purely semiotic or linguistic manner. It clearly implicates Rey in Leia and Han's romantic relationship, and thus holds out the possibility that she may very well be their child (i.e., the product of their love). If so, her relationship with Kylo Ren/Ben Solo becomes a kind of inverted analogue to the Luke-Leia relationship—twins separated at birth who are both strong with the Force but are unaware of their biological connection.

Second, by detaching from what was formerly a strict adherence to Han and Leia (with all its romantic/erotic associations), the leitmotif identifies Leia and Rey as central to the workings of the Force. They are the protagonists, the real heroines of the story. After all, most of the men have either gone missing (Luke), or been murdered (Han), or turned to the dark side (Ben). Thus, the music (along with the narrative trajectory of *Episode VII*) makes the somewhat progressive suggestion that the entire fate of the galaxy hinges upon these two women. And even more provocatively, it always has. The only difference is that we (and perhaps they too) can now hear what the music has been intimating all along.

Yet, given what we know about how filmmakers most often deploy the leitmotif, it may be that Abrams is offering up on the surface a conception of gender dynamics that is ultimately subverted by his use of the Williams score. Much like George Lucas before him, Abrams distributes the "Han and Leia" leitmotif across the film as an instrument of absolute signification—music as language. By doing so, he is indeed telegraphing to us a very clear message: "These women hold the key to the Force." And this would seem to be a fairly progressive shift in the *Star Wars* universe. But because of the way Williams develops (or fails to develop) this leitmotif in *The Force Awakens* (and throughout the *Star Wars* series as a whole), the end result may actually be regressive. If it is indeed a "derivative" figure that longs for its original, then it is only able to signal a return to what has already occurred. Which would mean that, try as they might, no one (neither Leia-Han-Rey nor Abrams) can escape the musical logic that will not allow any kind of substantive change or development. The audience too is caught up in the music's eternal return. If it seems like we've heard this all before, it's because we have—a long time ago in a galaxy far, far away.

But interpreting the music in *The Force Awakens* in a way that forecloses any potential for change or progress remains unsatisfying, in part because of the mythic nature of the leitmotif, which resists such a restrictive construal. Yes, music clarifies the inner properties of the diegetic world, but insofar as it remains music, its very presence in the cinematic experience generates a fundamental sense of hiddenness and ambiguity. Thus, it seems reasonable to suggest that the origin to which the leitmotif is "returning" is one that was always already there to begin with but we simply didn't have the ears to hear. It's a primal story in which women (first Amidala, then Leia, and now Rey) have always been the central figures.

Could it be that the whole *Star Wars* mythology is in fact an origin story about strong women and their mothers, not whiny little boys with daddy (and grand-daddy) issues? And is it possible that, only now, with an ever-expanding musical canvas of potentially infinite films do we have the necessary space to allow this mythic reality to be fully realized? Perhaps. Or perhaps not. Deciding one way or the other is, in a very real sense, a matter of interpretation. It's also part of the fun.

Still, not all interpretations are created equal. For instance, the numerous fans who complained about Leia snubbing Chewbacca had every right to respond to a scene that they perceived to be problematic. But the unsettling nature of the scene actually has very little to do with the emotional state of a Wookiee. Rather, it has everything to do with the radical shift within the mythic substrate of the *Star Wars* universe that takes place when Leia hugs Rey—a gendered shift carried almost entirely by the film's music. And while the shared intuition of the fan-base proved correct (i.e., something doesn't feel quite right about this scene!), they misunderstood the depth of their collective insight. For it isn't simply that Chewbacca has no one to comfort him (again, he's a Wookiee; he'll be ok). It is rather that the audience's gendered expectations (i.e., hetero-normative masculinity) are subverted by the music. In the process, that which filmgoers have internalized and thus failed to recognize is suddenly revealed. Because it so often functions as a linguistic signifier, the Han and Leia leitmotif threatens to negate the narrative's forward progress by returning viewers to a primordial past. But because it is music, it has the capacity to negate that negation, opening up interpretive possibilities that would otherwise remain inaccessible and, quite literally, unheard of.

Bibliography

Adorno, W. Theodor. *In Search of Wagner.* Translated by Rodney Livingstone. London: Verso, 1989.

Adorno, W. Theodor, and Hans Eisler. *Composing for the Films.* London: Athlone, 1994.

Bricken, Rob. "J. J. Abrams admits lying about Star Trek 2's Khan was a mistake." *Gizmodo,* December 2, 2013. http://io9.gizmodo.com/j-j-abrams-admits-lying-about-star-trek-2s-khan-was-a-1475078061.

Brooker, Will. *Using the Force: Creativity, Community and Star Wars Fans.* New York: Penguin, 2002.

Buhler, James. "*Star Wars,* Music, and Myth." In *Music and Cinema,* edited by James Buhler, et al., 33–57. Middletown, CT: Wesleyan University Press, 2000.

Callaway, Kutter. *Scoring Transcendence: Film Music as Contemporary Religious Experience.* Waco, TX: Baylor University Press, 2012.

Cavelos, Jeanne. "Stop Her, She's Got a Gun! How the Rebel Princess and the Virgin Queen Became Marginalized and Powerless in George Lucas's Fairy Tale." In *Star Wars on Trial: Science Fiction and Fantasy Writers Debate the Most Popular Science Fiction Films of All Time,* edited by Jeanne Cavelos and Bill Spangler, 305–22. Dallas: Benbella, 2006.

Chiusano, Scott. "J. J. Abrams Answers Questions about Leia and Rey Hug in 'The Force Awakens,' Says It Wasn't His Intention to 'Slight' Chewbacca." *New York Daily News,* March 9, 2016. http://www.nydailynews.com/entertainment/movies/abrams-explains-leia-rey-hug-force-awakens-article-1.2558239.

Cranny-Francis, Ann. "Feminist Futures: A Generic Study." In *Alien Zone: Cultural Theory and Contemporary Science Fiction Cinema,* edited by Annette Kuhn, 219–27. London: Verso, 1990.

Dominguez, Diana. "Feminism and the Force: Empowerment and Disillusionment in a Galaxy Far, Far Away." In *Culture, Identities, and Technology in the Star Wars Films: Essays on the Two Trilogies*, edited by Carl Silvio and Tony M. Vinci, 109–33. Jefferson, NC: McFarland, 2007.

Jenkins, Henry. *Convergence Culture: Where Old and New Media Collide*. New York: New York University Press, 2006.

Lyden, John C. "The More Things Change: Historical Political Context and *The Force Awakens*." In *The Myth Awakens: Canon, Conservatism, and Fan Reception of* Star Wars, edited by Ken Derry and John Lyden, 23–32. Eugene, OR: Cascade, 2018.

McDowell, John C. *Identity Politics in George Lucas' Star Wars*. Jefferson, NC: McFarland, 2016.

Mittell, Jason. *Complex TV: The Poetics of Contemporary Television Storytelling*. New York: New York University Press, 2015.

Sciretta, Peter. "Exclusive: J. J. Abrams Explains Why Leia's Hug in 'The Force Awakens' Was Probably a 'Mistake.'" *SlashFilm*, March 8, 2016. http://www.slashfilm.com/leia-hugging-rey-jj-abrams-force-awakens.

CHAPTER 5

THE RACISM AWAKENS

DANIEL WHITE HODGE AND JOSEPH BOSTON

Abstract: While *Star Wars* might be regarded as post-racial given the multiple species represented in the films, upon the release of the eagerly awaited first teaser trailer for *The Force Awakens* there was a significant racist backlash on social media with the revelation that actor John Boyega would have a major role as ex-storm trooper Finn. This reaction may have been a result of casting a Black man as a substantial character in the series who: 1) does not die early; 2) does not have a background role like Lando Calrissian; and 3) is not representative of the *Star Wars* universe in which the diversity of alien species clearly overshadows the diversity of human ethnicities. This chapter seeks to explore the transmediation of race in two recent additions to the *Star Wars* franchise, *The Force Awakens* (2015) and *Rogue One* (2016). We will briefly historicize the images of Black characters in Hollywood. Then, using a qualitative ethno-media analysis, we will examine: 1) *Star Wars* fandom response to Finn; 2) the role of Finn in *The Force Awakens*; and 3) the racial overtones within *Rogue One*.

There is no argument that the *Star Wars* film sagas, including the Expanded Universe segments, are both an economic powerhouse and a socio-mythological narrative within the American pantheon. Moreover, they provide a Western-hero-storyline, which many millions of people identify with passionately. *Star Wars* fandom in fact represents a myriad of entities, cultures, countries, and ethnicities. In this regard, *Star Wars* could be considered a "post-racial" film saga. However, upon the release of *The Force Awakens'* eagerly awaited, and secretly kept, trailer, the social media world seemed to implode on itself when seeing a Black[1] actor, John Boyega, play the role of Finn—a substantial character in the new saga who: 1) does not die early; 2) does not have a background role like that of Lando Calrissian (played by Billy Dee Williams); and 3) is not representative of the *Star Wars* universe in which the diversity of alien species clearly overshadows the diversity of human ethnicities. In connection to this last point, many *Star Wars* fans reacted to the character of Finn with outright racism. Their responses ranged from referring to Finn as a "space nigger,"[2] to calling for boycotts of the film, to asserting that the stormtroopers needed to be "all White."[3] So. What might have caused this reaction? Had the *Star Wars* universe stumbled upon a Force that it could not explain or control? Was it J. J. Abrams's intention to mar *Star Wars* with racial overtones and intersectionalities of race, gender, and class? Did he have a much larger plan?

Hollywood has had a long-time problem with the issues of race and ethnicity.[4] From Mickey Rooney playing a brutal stereotype of Asians in *Breakfast At Tiffany's* (1961) to the portrayal of Moses by Charlton Heston, an American of British background, Hollywood has continually signaled that Whites are dominant in all regards in part by ensuring that ethnic minorities have very little representation on screen. In contrast to this pattern, J. J. Abrams stood out by casting Boyega in a lead role in *Star Wars: The Force Awakens*. Abrams appeared to be sending a message that a Black man and a White woman can save the universe just as well as, say, a blond blue-eyed Skywalker. It was noteworthy to see a Black storm trooper—especially one that defects. And to have a woman who is skilled

1. We have used the term "Black" rather than "African American" to be more inclusive; in fact, John Boyega is himself British, and it is noteworthy that he does not use a British accent in the film, unlike Daisy Ridley who is also British but keeps her accent. Does this choice indicate that American audiences are confused if a Black person has a British accent, or seems to not be African American (the default Black person)? Are US audiences incapable of understanding that there are persons of color from all nations, with various accents? What stereotype is being supported here? Some controversy also followed Black British actor Daniel Kaluuya in his portrayal of an African American in *Get Out* (2017), as Samuel L. Jackson criticized this casting decision, and Kaluuya responded. See Levy, "'Get Out' Star."

2. Post number 62965888 by Anonymous in "Star Wars Awakens First Clip."

3. Franich, "John Boyega."

4. For discussions of this issue see Kelley, *Race Rebels*; Neal, "Sold Out on Soul"; Wise, *Colorblind*.

with the Force is unprecedented in the *Star Wars* films up to this point. In addition, Gareth Edwards created an entire multi-ethnic narrative in *Rogue One* (2016), which sees a rebel unit led by a woman and Latinx take on the Empire. This was a definite uptick from earlier saga narratives. Still, the Racism Force was disturbed by these two films and it created a wrinkle in the imagination of many White audience members. When a power shift occurs in hegemonic structures, there is typically resistance.[5] Further, this type of resistance is a relic of something found in our universe much too often, yet hidden from view until something like this happens: a deep-seated hatred and fear of Blacks in positions of power.[6]

This chapter, therefore, seeks to explore the transmediation of race in the two new additions to the *Star Wars* film narrative, *The Force Awakens* (2015) and *Rogue One* (2016). We will briefly historicize the images of Black characters in Hollywood. Then, using a qualitative ethno-media analysis, we will examine: 1) *Star Wars* fandom responses to Finn; 2) the role of Finn in *The Force Awakes* and lastly; 3) the racial overtones within *Rogue One*.

Black Images in Film

The history of Black filmmakers' impact on the movie industry, and vice versa, has been well documented by African American scholars.[7] Aside from its obvious connections to discussions of race, this topic also involves considerations of sexuality, threat, and action on the silver screen. Black actors and actresses have had to overcome many hurdles, including being subjected to extreme racism, typecasting, and restricted to productions labeled "Black films" (and so relegated to a smaller market).[8] Moreover, in contrast to the multi-dimensional roles that White actors are allowed to play, Black actors have been limited to stereotypes or, even worse, roles that do not garner them a notice from the all-important Oscars. Roles such as Malcolm X played by Denzel Washington or even Taraji Henson's in *Hidden Figures* (2016) are often not seen as valuable or worthy of Hollywood's

5. Wise, *White Like Me*, 53–86.

6. Gormley, "The New-Brutality Film."

7. See Bogle, *Toms, Coons, Mulattoes*; Bonilla-Silva, *White Supremacy*; Boyd, *Am I Black Enough*; Donalson, *Black Directors*; Douglas, *What's Faith Got to Do with It?*; George, *Post-Soul Nation*; hooks, *Yearning*; Kelley, *Race Rebels*; Neal, "Sold out on Soul," *What the Music Said, Soul Babies*; West, *Race Matters*.

8. Boyd, *Am I Black Enough*.

highest reward. On the contrary, Denzel wins an Oscar for a crooked, thuggish police officer in *Training Day* (2001); Halle Berry wins for a sexual role in *Monster's Ball* (2001), in which she falls in love with a racist prison guard; and Mahershala Ali wins for portraying a drug dealer in *Moonlight* (2016). These roles all ring true to damaging tropes that have plagued African Americans in film for quite some time.

According to Donald Bogle, Black characters have had five foremost tropes in film.[9] These are:

1. *The Tom*: Acceptable good "Negro characters" yet continually harassed and hounded, as in James B. Lowe's role as the star of *Uncle Tom's Cabin* (1927).

2. *The Coon*: An amusement and "Black buffoon," which is represented by many different characters such as Uncle Remus in *The Green Pastures* (1936) and *Song of The South* (1946), and as recently as Marlon Wayans's character Ripcord in *G. I. Joe: The Rise of Cobra* (2009).

3. *The Tragic Mulatto*: A moviemaker's darling, the tragic mulatto is the "mixed" race character who is in trouble once his or her race is revealed. One of the earliest appearances of this trope was in *The Debt* (1912).

4. *The Mammy*: Related to comic coons, the mammy is usually big, fat, and cantankerous with a sassy wit about her. Many Black women have played this role; one of the most famous mammies was portrayed by Hattie McDaniel in *Gone with the Wind* (1939).

5. *The Brutal Black Buck*: Arguably one of the most powerful tropes of African Americans in film and seen throughout the gilded age of Hollywood, only to resurface during the 1970s, was the hard, tough, brutal, often violent, and menacing Black male. This trope was popularized in the infamous film by D. W. Griffith, *The Birth of a Nation* (1915).

These tropes have had an enormous impact on the ways in which audiences, especially Whites, have interpreted Black life and the African American experience. The power of media is immense; it shapes identity and how different groups view each other, and themselves. African Americans, among many other ethnic-minority groups, are in essence "created" through film

9. Adapted from Bogle, *Toms, Coons, Mulattoes*, 3–19.

and thereby assigned social roles by those images given to them by directors, who are, many times, White men.[10] Bogle adds,

> Once the basic mythic types were introduced, a number of things
> occurred. Specific black themes soon emerged. (The Old South
> theme proved to be a great favorite.) And the basic types came
> and went in various guises. . . . If a black appeared as a butler,
> audiences thought of him as merely a servant. What they failed
> to note was the variety of servants. There were tom servants
> (faithful and submissive), coon servants (lazy and unreliable),
> and mammy servants, just to name a few. What has to be remem-
> bered is that the servant's uniform was the guise certain types
> wore during a given period. That way Hollywood would give its
> audience the same product (the types themselves) but with new
> packaging (the guise).[11]

Using Bogle's tropes, we now have a foundation from which to examine
Star Wars' racial overtones.

Star Wars Fandom Responses to Finn

You would have thought that God had rewritten the Bible and had now
made up with Satan. *Star Wars* fan responses were an intriguing form of
racism to watch. For many years racism had not been a topic of discussion
regarding *Star Wars*, outside of the very limited use of Black characters by
Lucas in the original trilogy and prequels. But when the first trailers for *The
Force Awakens* began to emerge in 2014, some members of the *Star Wars*
fan base simply lost their racial minds. Responses varied, but it was clear

10. George, *Post-Soul Nation*; hooks, *Yearning*; Kelley, *Race Rebels*; Neal, *Soul Babies*; West, *Race Matters*; Wise, *White Like Me*.

11. Bogle, *Toms, Coons, Mulattoes*, 17–18. In a 1968 interview with Alex Haley, Jim
Brown similarly remarked on the power of movies to shape (self-)perceptions of African
Americans: "There's a crying need for more Negro actors, because for so long, ever since
the silent screen, in fact, the whole world has been exposed to Negroes in stereotype
roles. Have you ever been to any Negro theater with a movie going, with a Negro in it?
Well, you can just feel the tension of that audience, pulling for this guy to do something
good, something that will give them a little pride. That's why I feel so good that Negroes
are finally starting to play roles that other Negroes, watching, will feel proud of, and
respond to, and identify with, and feel real about, instead of being crushed by some Uncle
Tom on the screen making a fool of himself. You're not going to find any of us playing
Uncle Toms anymore." (Brown, "Alex Haley.")

that something had been jarred loose in the fan base upon seeing a Black man as a storm trooper. Some responses were:

- "Why are there Black storm troopers?"[12]

- "I'm not racist . . . but it just looks out of place."[13]

- "[*The Force Awakens*] puts minorities and women incessantly and ridiculously in your face to make a *political point* (not tell a story)."[14]

These comments are micro-aggressive in nature and represent the growing racial divide in the US. Yet, there was something even larger happening here. The canon was disturbed. The image of Whiteness as ruler, king, and chief intelligence was now shook and the creation of a Black storm trooper fractured the image of pureness within the *Star Wars* mythic pantheon. *Star Wars* in many ways is a sacred text; therefore it stands to reason that many, particularly Whites, are upset when the hallowed scrolls are disturbed with race. Social media sites like Twitter had the following:

This comment was similar to many others and the hashtag #BoycottStarWarsVII gained traction. Others joined in:

12. Comment by ChesterAnthem in "'Star Wars' Writers' Anti-Trump Rants."
13. "Review 73."
14. Brown, "Why Star Wars."

Responses like these echo the political correctness push-back that typically arises within right-wing conservative spaces that reject any form of diversity or "multiculturalism" that is not White. Further, these responses are also closely related to the resistance to the looming demographic changes happening throughout the US, a resistance upon which Donald Trump built a large part of his rhetoric during the 2016 election season.

Of course not all responses were racially charged. As seen in the image below, there were those who defended the notion of a Black storm trooper and pushed back on the racist tweets.

Not everyone in the *Star Wars* universe was disturbed by Finn, obviously. It is important to note that. Still, the point remains that the White canon of *Star Wars* was upset and the racialized push-back was clear. Finn being Black seems like an insignificant thing, but a Black role that is prominent and (marginally) non-stereotypical, in such a huge franchise as *Star Wars*, created a type of racist response that bears noting and exploring. This role seems to have shaken the racism of many *Star Wars* fans awake—but it was really awake the whole time.

Finn and The Racialized Force

Finn's character is one that, on the surface, may provide a refreshing "post-racial" sense of comfort to many. Such a view illustrates the desire and myth of a post-racial society erroneously thought by some to have been ushered in by the election of Barack Obama in 2008.[15] But it is a failed myth and one that continually needs interrogation and deconstruction. Given the fan response to Finn, things are not post-racial. In fact, his role in many regards is troubling, at the very least, as he is similar to both a Coon and a Tom under Bogle's tropes.

When Finn is first introduced, we are unaware of who he is because he is still wearing the storm trooper helmet. But something is different about this trooper because he is hesitant to murder anyone. When what appears to be a colleague of his is killed in front of him, leaving him with the distinguishing three blood marks, we really wonder who this is. It is then later revealed to the audience that FN-2187 is having second thoughts about the First Order and its intentions. He is able to ward off the heavy socialization towards compliance and submission to the Order along with making a heroic escape—all great things, on their own. But unfortunately there are many problems with Finn's character and story arc.

First, FN-2187 is renamed by Poe Dameron, played by Oscar Isaac. This is a strong reference back to the enslavement period when Whites would rename their African slaves to their liking. Histories were lost, family genealogies were gone, and identity was reshaped in the image of Whiteness. Finn, as his new name would come to be, allows himself to be renamed rather than taking a name for himself. After crashing on the desert planet Jakku he develops an unbearable thirst, to the point that we see him drink out of the same trough as an alien reptile-like beast. One can

15. For a discussion of this myth see Ledwidge et al., *Barack Obama*.

only imagine the stench and filth that is in that trough. This scene is also reminiscent of enslavement times when Africans were given the very worst of food, accommodations, and basic life essentials. Moreover, Finn at this point is still subject to the authority of someone else—Rey—rather than pursuing the liberty and freedom he initiated.

Second, as Finn continues on, he is almost child-like in his approach to war and weapons. For someone who has been literally raised in the military, he appears to barely know how to dress himself, comically stumbling through attempts to put on his storm trooper suit. He is overly excited—dare I say Coon like—when he first takes out a target, and later in the film defers to a rebel, who has apparently not had First Order weapons training. To make matters worse, we come to find out that Finn was part of the sanitation detail while stationed on the First Order base—a janitor. This revelation has all types of racialized implications to it, sending us back to the 1930s in film when African Americans were just in the background, part of the "help."[16] In this same way Finn is not able to come up with a proper plan of attack although the White man, Han Solo, is. Once again all the "smart ones" are White males, and Blacks are just there to offer assistance.

Third, Finn has cowardly traits. For most of the film he is afraid to confront the First Order and wants only to run away. Sometimes these attempts, as when he and Rey first meet while trying to avoid being killed in the Jakku market, are actually played for humor, positioning Finn again as comic relief. While it is true that someone looking for freedom will do anything they can to avoid being enslaved again, Finn has no fight in him until the very end. Finn's cowardice is similar to the long-standing stereotype that African Americans are lazy, idle by nature, and lethargic towards any form of work—especially patriotism. Yes, it is true that Finn is the one who leads the raid on Star Killer base to save Rey. But it is almost out of character for him to do so by that point in the film.

Fourth, and lastly, Finn is literally asleep for the climax of the story. He is not even present to partake in what is typically the most important part of any film. Finn might as well have died (following another standard Hollywood trope for Black characters) for all that he contributes to the finale. In this regard Andre Seewood asserts:

> The Finn character, from the moment we saw him as the first image in the original trailer, to the moment he was knocked unconscious and remained unconscious throughout the final act of the

16. Donalson, *Black Directors*; Bogle, *Toms, Coons, Mulattoes*.

film, is a manifestation of what I will call: Hyper-tokenism in the White film.

Hyper-tokenism in a White film can be defined as the marked increase in screen time, dramatic involvement and promotional images of a Black character in a White film, while simultaneously reserving full dramatic agency as the providence of White characters by the end of the film.[17]

Finn sleeps through the ending of the film,
while Rey prepares to search for Luke.

Finn's role is just that, a hyper-tokenistic character that offers only a wink towards interculturalism. Finn appears to be nothing more than a desired effect for trailers and marketing. Seewood once again states,

> The battle for racial inclusiveness and equality in the cinema begins and ends with the degree of dramatic agency that is shared among characters of different races and genders within a film's story. Black representation in White film must not solely be based on the presence of a Black actor or actors within that White film, but instead we have to understand that it is the degree of dramatic agency that the Black character wields within the context of the White film that ultimately determines whether that Black actor is used as a token or as a fully realized dramatic entity.[18]

As Seewood correctly points out, Finn absolutely lacks dramatic agency in *The Force Awakens*, and as such he clearly stands as a mere token.

17. Seewood, "Hyper-Tokenism."
18. Ibid.

Professor Stacy L. Smith conducted a study in 2016 that was believed to be the largest intersectional analysis of characters in the motion picture industry to date. This study revealed that "Hollywood is an epicenter of cultural inequality." Only 26.3 percent of all roles in films went to non-White actors, for example, while 31.4 percent of speaking roles went to girls and women.[19] Smith states, "While the voices calling for change have escalated in number and volume there is little evidence that this has transformed the movies that we see and the people hired to create them. Our reports demonstrate that the problems are pervasive and systemic."[20] This finding of course applies to one of cinema's most enduring and top grossing franchises of all time, *Star Wars*. Casting is important to any film but in terms of profit, *Star Wars* might be the only franchise where casting doesn't matter because regardless of who you hire, the film is going to do incredible box office numbers.

The casting of the largely unknown Daisy Ridley, an English actress whose previous work has been in bit parts in various TV shows and films, highlights the ongoing misogynoir inherent to the *Star Wars* universe and the problem Hollywood has with Black women. An inexperienced actress is given a central role while Oscar winner Lupita Nyong'o is relegated to a supporting CGI character (Maz Kanata). This is simply the latest example of Hollywood's misogynoir and its "problem" with Black women writ large. We have been treated to token nods to Black characters in the six films, who are all men: Lando, Mace Windu, and now Finn. But where are the Black women? Apparently, they do not exist in the present, future, or in galaxies far, far away. Why not Lupita Nyong'o as the heroine of *The Force Awakens*? Because even in an imagined universe, a racist, anti-Black, misogynoirist Hollywood has difficulty appreciating a Black women's humanity, which is why Nyong'o is in the background and embodied as alien, as other.

Where is the venerated meritocracy so touted by Hollywood liberals in the casting of Daisy Ridley as one of the main protagonists "Rey" while Lupita Nyong'o is disembodied as a minor background character after winning the highest honor one can receive in the profession of acting? One supposes Nyong'o should just be happy with the "boobie prize" of couture magazine covers where White people apparently have just discovered that Black women too are beautiful? This is another example of the fallacy of meritocracy where "Whiteness" trumps "merit" and carries more value

19. "Hollywood Equality."
20. Ibid.

and currency than any award (even the highest honor in your field) could confer to a Black person. And so the question remains: Where are the Black women in *Star Wars*?

A Resistance Built on Race?

While having a White female lead is a changing of the guard, so to speak, this decision is not as groundbreaking as it might at first appear, particularly when one takes into account the legacy of Carrie Fisher's Leia to the franchise. What would have been truly revolutionary in *The Force Awakens* and *Rogue One* is a Black woman as protagonist, as Rey or as Jyn Erso. For all intents and purposes, Erso is a Black woman on the run from the Empire in the vein of an Assata Shakur or Angela Davis. Her father is a scientist kidnapped by the state as an unwilling participant, leaving his daughter to the tender care of a Black resistance fighter who is deemed even too extreme by the Rebel Alliance's standards. The questions about why Erso was cast as a White woman in a film apparently centered on diversity are as relevant to this discourse as to the reasons why a Black woman has yet to be cast as the lead in a *Star Wars* film.

The problematic ethos of *Rogue One* is clearly articulated by director Gareth Edwards in an interview with *IndieWire*:

> It's been very easy in the past to label it as we're the good guys and they're the bad guys . . . And the goal of a lot of films used to be: If we just eliminate the bad guy, we win. But I think a more modern, realistic viewpoint is that no one's good, no one's evil and the only real way we're going to stop wars is to understand each other better, come together and empathize with them. And this film tried to take away the black and white and make it more gray. You even see the point of view of the bad guys and you start to understand what [the Empire] tried to do.[21]

These comments are particularly troubling in light of the recent discourse on the divisiveness of "identity politics" after the 2016 election of President Donald Trump, with White liberals expressing a similar desire for People of Color to break bread with racists who see them as less than human.[22] This

21. Desowitz, "Rogue One."

22. The point here is to win over the Trump-supporting White voters who feel disenfranchised in order to return power to the Democrats. As Linda Burnham explains: "The controversy focuses on the role of 'identity politics' in Hillary Clinton's presidential

comparison to the election is not an idle one. A few days after the results of November 7 Chris Weitz, one of the writers of *Rogue One*, tweeted: "Please note that the Empire is a White supremacist (human) organization." His co-author Gary Whitta added that, in their film, this organization is "opposed by a multicultural group led by brave women."[23] Weitz and Whitta would appear to be less interested in the Empire's point of view than Edwards but they also remain apparently unaware of the various ways in which *Star Wars* reinscribes White supremacy, such as its continued failure to imagine a Black woman as protagonist. Not incidentally, no *Star Wars* film has ever had a director of color; those in charge of the franchise continue to represent the status quo in filmmaking, as in our society.

White supremacy in *Star Wars* is enacted not only by denying Black characters a central role in the films, but by undermining them when they do appear: Lando is a traitor, Finn is a coward, and Lupita Nyong'o is buried under latex. In *Rogue One* a similar dynamic is set up by first emphasizing Jyn Erso's self-centered privilege and her refusal to fight. When asked by Saw Gerrera, "You can stand to see the Imperial flag reign across the galaxy?," Jyn replies: "It's not a problem if you don't look up." Only when her father is killed and she becomes personally invested does Jyn advocate for an attack on Scarif to retrieve the plans for the Death Star. It is at this critical point that a Black woman finally makes a token appearance in the character of Senator Tynnra Pamlo, played by actress Sharon Duncan Brewster. In a meeting of the Rebel Alliance regarding what should be done about the Empire and its fearsome new weapon the Death Star, Senator Pamlo advocates that they should all run for their lives: "If the Empire has this kind of power, what chance do we have?" Jyn's response shows how completely she has moved away from her former position of non-intervention, and come into her own as a Joan of Arc archetype: "What chance do we have? The

---

defeat. Essentially, the debate turns on whether the Democratic party and Clinton, in their embrace of racial, religious and sexual minorities, forsook working-class white people, who responded to their abandonment by casting their votes for Trump. According to this perspective, the journey back from the devastation of 2016 requires that the party take an indefinite break from identity politics to concentrate on winning back economically squeezed white workers." (Burnham, "Liberals." See also Kim and Camacho, "God Is a Neoliberal Centrist.")

23. Sims, "A Deleted Tweet." Note that Weitz soon deleted his tweet and apologized for politicizing the film. Many White supremacists agreed with his allegory (if not his politics), however, and said that instead of boycotting the film entirely they would watch it and cheer for the Empire. As one commented: "If you're like me you'll pirate [*Rogue One*] at some point and fantasize about being a stormtrooper" (Calvario, "Rogue One").

question is what choice? Run? Hide? Plead for mercy? Scatter your forces? You give way to an enemy this evil with this much power and you condemn the galaxy to an eternity of submission. The time to fight is now!"

Jyn Erso and Tynnra Pamlo. One of these women wants to fight, and one wants to run away. It matters which is which.

While the Rebel Alliance sides with Palmo, it is ultimately the rebellion against the Rebellion by a White female protagonist that leads to the attack on Scarif and the retrieval of the Death Star plans. This development highlights the issues that Hollywood filmmakers continue to have in portraying Black people with agency, instead of consistently defaulting to a White Savior trope in which White characters, whether male or female, are more competent, heroic, and skilled than their Black counterparts. While *Rogue One* has a cast of diverse faces at the center and foreground of its narrative, Black faces are erased or denied agency by White leadership. Instead we are offered token representations of Black characters like Finn and Palmo saying "RUN," while White people save the day.[24]

After handing over the *Star Wars* franchise to Disney for a reported $4 billion in 2012, George Lucas ironically (and infamously) stated in an interview with Charlie Rose that he felt like he had "sold [his kids] off to the white slavers."[25] The implication is that Lucas thinks of this franchise as Black in some respect, despite the fact that there has been no real Black protagonist in any of the films, and no Black creator making them. At no point under Lucas, and now under Disney, has anyone been willing to hand over the future of *Star Wars* to Black actors and directors. This point applies even in *Rogue One*, when the story would arguably make more narrative and historical sense if Jyn Erso was Black. *Star Wars* is a forty-year long production that instills ideas of Empire, Whiteness, and Patriarchy, passed from generation to generation. Indeed "the Force" that controls this process is White Privilege, and it "is with you" both in the film and the real world, giving power or taking it away—all depending on the color of your skin.

---

24. This approach is consistently the default for Hollywood even when it's unnecessary or when a film is based on real events, as in the case of the hugely successful *Hidden Figures* (2016). The film's director, Theodore Melfi, wrote in a White Savior character played by Kevin Costner, who helps to desegregate the workplace toilets by smashing down the "Colored Ladies Room" sign. In fact no such person existed, and it was Katherine Johnson who refused to so much as enter the colored bathrooms. When asked why he wrote in this scene, Melfi responded that he didn't see a problem with adding a white hero into the story and that, "There needs to be white people who do the right thing and there needs to be black people who do the right thing. . . . And so who cares who does the right thing, as long as the right thing is achieved." (Thomas, "Space So White.") But why do there need to be White people doing "the right thing" in a story that is ostensibly about systemic racism and oppression? Apparently to soothe the consciences of White audiences.

25. Trendacosta, "A Not-So-Brief History."

Concluding Thoughts

Discussions of transmediated images of race in film are complicated and often messy. The ongoing dilemma of racial representation in Hollywood film will not be solved anytime soon. However, this fact does not mean that those of us who are avid filmgoers should displace our critical eye and avoid the issue altogether. In truth, it becomes an even greater responsibility of the viewer to speak up and act on the issue. We are making the case in this chapter that we need a much more critical interpretive lens when watching films and considering the importance of race, even—perhaps especially—in those films that appear to be racially tolerant.

Star Wars is a global franchise that has the hearts, minds, and wallets of many. The issues that we raise in this chapter should begin a much deeper conversation on how we think about race within sacred film canons such as Star Wars. Race cannot be avoided. As mythic and wondrous as the Star Wars saga may be, we have to keep in mind that White men still control most of the decision-making in Hollywood. And while there is some movement that is giving a voice to more Black films, such as Moonlight (2016), the road is still a long and narrow one towards equality and impartiality in casting and narrative. Our hope as authors is to have provoked a discussion that takes us further into the issue of race while still keeping in mind the positive mythical components of such a great film saga as Star Wars. May the (non-racialized) Force be with us all in that journey!

Bibliography

Bogle, Donald. *Toms, Coons, Mulattoes, Mammies and Bucks: An Interpretive History of Blacks in American Films*. New York: Continuum, 2000.

Bonilla-Silva, Eduardo. *White Supremacy and Racism in the Post-Civil Rights Era*. Boulder, CO: L. Rienner, 2001.

Boyd, Todd. *Am I Black Enough for You? Popular Culture from the 'Hood and Beyond*. Indianapolis: Indiana University Press, 1997.

Brown, David G. "Why Star Wars: The Force Awakens Is a Social Justice Propaganda Film." *Return of Kings*, 2015. http://www.returnofkings.com/75991/why-star-wars-the-force-awakens-is-a-social-justice-propaganda-film.

Brown, Jim. "Alex Haley Interviews Jim Brown." *Playboy*, February 1968. http://www.alex-haley.com/alex_haley_jim_brown_interview.htm.

Burnham, Linda. "Liberals, Don't Fall into the Right's 'Identity Politics' Trap." *The Guardian*, February 10, 2017. https://www.theguardian.com/commentisfree/2017/feb/10/liberals-right-identity-politics-progressive.

Calvario, Liz. "'Rogue One': White Supremacists Call for Boycott of 'Star Wars' Film Over 'Anti-White Agenda.'" *IndieWire*, December 7, 2016. http://www.indiewire.com/2016/12/rogue-one-white-supremacists-boycott-star-wars-film-anti-white-agenda-1201753703.

Desowitz, Bill. "'Rogue One': How Gareth Edwards Made a Gritty 'Star Wars' Movie About Diversity." *IndieWire*. December 5, 2016. http://www.indiewire.com/2016/12/rogue-one-star-wars-gareth-edwards-interview-1201752554.

Donalson, Melvin Burke. *Black Directors in Hollywood*. Austin, TX: University of Texas Press, 2003.

Douglas, Kelly Brown. *What's Faith Got to Do with It? Black Bodies/Christian Souls*. Maryknoll, NY: Orbis, 2005.

Franich, Darren. "John Boyega Tells Racist 'Star Wars' Fans to 'Get Used to It.'" *Entertainment Weekly*, December 1, 2014. http://ew.com/article/2014/12/01/john-boyega-black-stormtrooper-star-wars.

George, Nelson. *Post-Soul Nation: The Explosive, Contradictory, Triumphant, and Tragic 1980s as Experienced by African Americans (Previously Known as Blacks and Before That Negroes)*. New York: Viking, 2004.

Gormley, Paul. *The New-Brutality Film: Race and Affect in Contemporary Hollywood Cinema*. Bristol, UK: Intellect, 2005.

"Hollywood Equality: All Talk, Little Action." *USC Annenberg School for Communication and Journalism*, September 6, 2016. http://annenberg.usc.edu/news/faculty-research/hollywood-equality-all-talk-little-action.

hooks, bell. *Yearning: Race, Gender, and Cultural Politics*. Boston: South End, 1990.

Kelley, Robin D. G. *Race Rebels: Culture, Politics, and the Black Working Class*. New York: Free, 1994.

Kim, Grace Ji-Sun, and Daniel José Camacho. "God Is a Neoliberal Centrist." *Time*, July 29, 2016. http://time.com/4430635/god-neoliberal-centrist.

Ledwidge, Mark, et al. *Barack Obama and the Myth of a Post-Racial America*. New York: Routledge, 2014.

Levy, Dani. "'Get Out' Star Daniel Kaluuya on Samuel L. Jackson's Comments: 'I Resent That I Have to Prove I'm Black.'" *Variety*, May 14, 2017. http://variety.com/2017/film/news/get-out-daniel-kaluuya-samuel-l-jackson-black-british-actors-1202008756.

Neal, Mark Anthony. "Sold out on Soul: The Corporate Annexation of Black Popular Music." *Popular Music and Society* 21:3 (Fall 1997) 117–35.

———. *Soul Babies: Black Popular Culture and the Post-Soul Aesthetic*. New York: Routledge, 2002.

———. *What the Music Said: Black Popular Music and Black Public Culture*. New York: Routledge, 1999.

"Review 73: Star Wars: Episode VII: The Force Awakens." *The Critical Mormon vs. Hollywood*, March 10, 2016. https://themormoncritic.wordpress.com/2016/03/10/review-73-star-wars-episode-vii-the-force-awakens-15.

Seewood, Andre. "Hyper-Tokenism: 'The Force Awakens' While the Black Man Sleeps." *IndieWire*, December 23, 2015. http://www.indiewire.com/2015/12/hyper-tokenism-the-force-awakens-while-the-black-man-sleeps-162287.

Sim, Gerald. *The Subject of Film and Race: Retheorizing Politics, Ideology, and Cinema*. New York: Bloomsbury, 2014.

Sims, David. "A Deleted Tweet Won't Hurt *Rogue One*." *The Atlantic*, November 21, 2016. https://www.theatlantic.com/entertainment/archive/2016/11/the-inevitable-politicization-of-star-wars-rogue-one/508358.

"Star Wars Force Awakens First Clip." *4Archive* 2.5. https://4archive.org/board/tv/thread/62963221.

"'Star Wars Writers' Anti-Trump Rants May Hurt 'Rogue One' at the Box Office." *Reddit*. https://www.reddit.com/r/The_Donald/comments/5f2im2/star_wars_writers_antitrump_rants_may_hurt_rogue.

Thomas, Dexter. "Space So White." *Vice*, January 25, 2017. https://news.vice.com/story/oscar-nominated-hidden-figures-was-whitewashed-but-it-didnt-have-to-be.

Trendacosta, Katharine. "A Not-So-Brief History of George Lucas Talking Shit about Disney's Star Wars." io9, December 31, 2015. http://io9.gizmodo.com/a-not-so-brief-history-of-george-lucas-talking-shit-abo-1750464055.

West, Cornel. *Race Matters*. Boston: Beacon, 1993.

Wise, Tim J. *Colorblind: The Rise of Post-Racial Politics and the Retreat from Racial Equity*. San Francisco: City Lights, 2010.

———. *White Like Me: Reflections on Race from a Privileged Son*. Rev. ed. Brooklyn: Soft Skull, 2008.

CHAPTER 6

DO, OR DO NOT: THERE IS NO TRY

Race, Rhetoric, and Diversity in
the *Star Wars* Universe

JOSHUA CALL

Abstract: One of the great virtues of myth-making, whether ancient or contemporary, is the ability to recognize oneself in the story being told. Indeed, this recognition is necessary in order for myths to maintain their power. Popular culture myths, and fandoms more specifically, rely on this same practice in equally necessary ways. It provides the backbone for the immersive nature of the experience. This level of immersion, when done well, moves fluidly across racial and gendered boundaries. *Star Wars* as a fandom has long embraced this practice through its Expanded Universe, particularly in games. Unfortunately, the framing narratives of the principle canon in the *Star Wars* universe (namely the franchise films) has been less adept at recognizing and embracing the generative and rhetorical power of myth-making that has so captured *Star Wars* fandom. To explore the rhetorical differences in identification means to analyze the distancing effects of racial marking in *The Force Awakens* when compared to the immersive—and arguably more inclusive—tropes employed by the Expanded Universe.

Introduction

Oⁿe of the great virtues of myth-making, whether ancient or contemporary, is the ability to recognize oneself in the story being told.
Indeed, this recognition is necessary in order for myths to maintain their
power; prescience is predicated on perception. Popular culture myths, and
fandoms more specifically, rely on this same practice in equally necessary
ways. It provides the backbone for the immersive nature of the experience.
This level of immersion, when done well, moves fluidly across racial and
gendered boundaries. *Star Wars* as a fandom has long embraced this practice through its Expanded Universe of graphic novels, animation, cosplay,
and games. Unfortunately, the framing narratives of the principal canon in
the *Star Wars* universe (namely the franchise films) have been less adept at
recognizing and embracing the generative and rhetorical power of myth-
making that has so captured the *Star Wars* fandom. This chapter explores
the rhetorical differences in this phenomenon of identification by analyzing the distancing effects of racial marking in *The Force Awakens* when
compared to the immersive, and arguably more inclusive tropes employed
by *Star Wars* games in the Expanded Universe.

Myth-making and Identification

Examining the *Star Wars* universe through a lens of mythology is both complicated and compelling. Nevertheless, to the degree to which myth-making
is about storytelling as a kind of moralistic meaning-making, *Star Wars* can
and should be read with some of the lenses that mythology affords. As a
text, though, the *Star Wars* franchise more generally, and the initial three
films more specifically, have the unique quality of being a myth crafted particularly to match Joseph Campbell's model of the monomyth. Many critics
and scholars have used the lens of the monomyth to articulate the moral
spectrum of characters in *Star Wars* films,[1] by offering a careful read of what
the thematic elements of the Force can teach readers/viewers about the
scope of moral decision making. Indeed, the fascination that Lucas held for
Campbell's work, and his own admission that the original trilogy was crafted
specifically with the hero's journey in mind, suggest a particular approach
to reading the text. Still, while much has been made of the monomythic

---

1. E.g., Gordon, "*Star Wars*"; Lyden, "The Apocalyptic Cosmology of *Star Wars*";
and Peters, "The Force as Law."

structure as a framework for making meaning, it is the ways in which that structure functions as a rhetorically persuasive device that have bearing for a discussion of race and visibility in *The Force Awakens*.

Myths require the power of persuasion to be effective. Interestingly, their persuasive ability is effectively removed from their relative truth value. For Campbell and the monomythic structure specifically, the effects of myth are made tangible largely through Freudian analysis and Jungian archetypes.[2] The hero's journey effectively serves as a *bildungsroman*, mapping out a kind of experience with challenge and adversity. The hero functions as an idealized avatar, a semiotic or representative self responsible for exploring the possibilities of moral decision-making. This changes only slightly when applied to a heavily visual medium like *Star Wars*, due to the represented nature of characters. The visibility and viability of any particular character or representation hinges on the ability of that specific performance to communicate believability in the role. In this regard, character representations are rhetorical acts.

Kenneth Burke outlined an approach to persuasiveness in *A Rhetoric of Motives* that is particularly useful for exploring this relationship. Burke, who began his career primarily focused on literary experiences, later became enamored with the question of why literature was ultimately persuasive for readers. He argues that all persuasion, particularly in regards to the literary, hinges on an experience of identification that effectively bridges the divide between the audience and the speaker or text. For Burke, the power of rhetoric comes from the ability to create a shared sense or experience by seeing something of oneself in another to overcome our natural divisions. We have a desire to identify with others, to mitigate the ever-present sense that we are "both joined and separate, at once a distinct substance and consubstantial with another."[3] The rhetorical power of characters to sponsor this experience is expressed largely through the tropes and characteristics they represent, and how they "awaken an attitude of collaborative expectancy in us."[4] In effect, as we are presented with characters that have particular tropes and characteristics, and we are asked to engage and identify with those characters to the degree that they reflect characteristics and elements of our own experience and self-identity.

2. Campbell, *The Hero.*

3. Burke, *A Rhetoric of Motives*, 57.

4. Ibid., 58.

In the context of *Star Wars*, this means to recognize the ways in which characters intersect with the lived reality of the audience. The key element of Burke's framework lies in the ability of the rhetorical text to collapse the distance from the audience. To be persuaded by Luke Skywalker does not mean that a viewer must have some personal experience working moisture vaporators in a desert (although that experience might help), but rather the degree to which we can see what Luke's experiences mean: loneliness, isolation, a desire for greater and more important things. The degree to which we can participate in a shared sense of the value of these tropes is contingent on how we read the character's representation as being authentic and honest. This is ultimately where the film franchise of *Star Wars* has always struggled with representations of race.

The genre of science fiction has long been plagued by problematic rhetorical constructions of race. Isiah Lavender explores the history of science fiction and its troubling racial constructs by looking at how the genre embraces narratives involving race and power dynamics in human interactions. These narratives, though, often employ what he terms "Jim Crow extrapolations"[5] to highlight or resolve these complications. Science fiction narratives with exhaustive bio-diversity could seem to be rhetorically suggestive of genetic and racial inclusion, a mythology of diversity where the troubling realities of race are no longer present. The degree to which *Star Wars* specifically (or science fiction in general) is successful here is conditional on the degree to which characters persuasively communicate this reality.

The Force Awakens

The idea that "representation matters" is not a new one, and it's certainly not a new critique of *Star Wars* films. Not surprisingly, there is an equal amount of tension in the fandom when discussions of how *Star Wars* handles race emerge.

The central issue of racial visibility in the *Star Wars* universe lies with how race and related tropes inform the character and their interactions. We are regularly presented with an opulence of xeno-diversity. Even in the original trilogy, where practical effects limited the technical ability of rendering alien species, we see numerous examples of alien species. We see their representation increase through the original three films, arguably

5. Lavender, *Race in American Science Fiction*, 91.

a function of increased production budgets. Fast forward to the prequel films, and the addition of expansive CGI, and this becomes even more pronounced. The universe is alive with all variety of life. The characters of the films take this in stride, recognizing that they exist within this diversity. Even fresh-off-the-farm Luke Skywalker isn't terribly surprised by the presence of the Aquilash brute Ponda Baba during their confrontation in *A New Hope*. Instead, his reaction reads more like an inexperienced youth recognizing that he has just crossed the threshold into a more dangerous place than he knows how to navigate. Occasionally we might get a surprise reaction at the uniqueness or strangeness of a species, such as how an unnamed Imperial Officer is taken aback by the presence of the Trandoshan mercenary Bossk during *The Empire Strikes Back*, or Han Solo's brief surprise at being captured by the teddy-bear like Ewoks during *Return of the Jedi*. The message here is clear: the universe is a vast and distinct place, and differentiation across species is the galactic normal.

Given the great lengths the franchise has gone to show us the variety of species in the galaxy, it seems particularly striking that they are not as exhaustive at their representations within species, humanity in particular. The number of times we are presented with human characters of color are so few as to be singularly noteworthy. In the principal canon franchise, we have, broadly speaking, only four characters of color with any significant and obvious role in the plot. Lando Calrissian (played by Billy Dee Williams), represents the singular appearance of human racial diversity in the entire original trilogy. Mace Windu (played by Samuel L. Jackson), represents the sole significant character of color in the prequel films. One might be tempted to argue that the presence of Hugh Quarshie's Captain Panaka from *The Phantom Menace* and Jay Laga'aia as Captain Typho from *Attack of the Clones* represent a significant move forward. They might even be tempted to add that the presence of Temuera Morrison in *Clones* as both Jango Fett and the Clone Army characterizes significant advancement of visibility for actors of color relative to the story. Unfortunately, these characters represent singular appearances within individual films. Unlike Jackson and Williams, whose roles move beyond an individual film to impact the narrative framework in multiple iterations, by design characters of color are, as a whole, less visible, and less impactful in the *Star Wars* film universe. In this way, *Star Wars* has built itself on a history of tokenizing characters and caricatures that fail to provide any persuasive identification for diverse audiences. More problematically, viewers should consider if any of these characters genuinely represent positive inclusivity. Given the often-tokenizing nature of characters like Lando, Adilifu Nama posits the idea of "affirmative action sci-fi" where Black characters (and Black bodies) serve as a nod to "representational political correctness"[6] who function as an "oscillating state of race relations in American society."[7]

Because of this, many waited with anticipation for the arrival of the sequel films, that they might see a shift to a more diverse cast of characters; a new hope for the future of the franchise. For a moment, when the trailers for *The Force Awakens* were released, the presence of John Boyega's Finn as one of the most visible characters produced an explosion in the fan community. The sudden visibility of a Black man in what would be a significant role for the film represented a considerable departure for the franchise. Accordingly, the various factions of the fan community took to social media with a variety of responses, the most visible of which was an overwhelmingly negative, and racially charged boycott organized around the hashtag #BoycottStarWarsVII.[8] While the Twitter war around this issue seemed to largely rally those that were excited about Boyega's presence, the reaction nevertheless reflects an underlying reality about the franchise: diverse human bodies have not been visible. Writing for *The Guardian*, Steven Thrasher pens a moving account of why the early visibility of Finn was such a significant factor. His account focuses on childhood memories where, as a Black youth, he was always relegated to the role of being Lando Calrissian, with all the negative connotations that character carries simply because he was a Black body.[9] In contrast, the presence of Boyega's Finn was heralded as a new direction for inclusion and diverse representation. The actor himself, in an interview with *V Magazine* replied, "People of color and women are increasingly being shown on-screen. For things to be whitewashed just doesn't make sense."[10] It would seem the hopes of many fans were to be realized. Much of this buildup for the release of the film relies on constructing a rhetorical ethos designed to create an idea that the film would be more inclusive than previous iterations. Boyega as an actor, and

6. Nama, *Black Space*, 33.

7. Ibid., 41.

8. Lee, "Twitter Trolls." There have been similarly racist Twitter reactions to the character of Rose Tico, played by Kelly Marie Tran in the more recent film *The Last Jedi*. See Parry, "Kelly Marie Tran."

9. Thrasher, "Star Wars: A Salute to Black Stormtroopers."

10. Renshaw, "John Boyega."

his character by extension, are an embodied argument for diversification through identification. Because we have a compelling and dynamic Black character central to the film, filmmakers want the film to be seen as less racially problematic than previous installments. The success or failure of this argument hinges entirely on Finn, and the degree to which audiences can identify with, and are persuaded by, the representation. What makes this argument significant is its rhetorical positioning specifically in relationship to the history of whiteness in the franchise. That history is a function of memory, much like Thrasher's account of problematic representations of Blackness in the original trilogy. To overcome history in this case means to overcome memory, and that is a difficult argument to achieve.

With the release of *The Force Awakens*, many things became obvious. The familiar cornucopia of diverse species was quickly visible. Audiences were treated to a range of creatures and characters from across the galaxy. There was an extended scene involving a cantina as a refuge for all the galaxy's oddities and variety. Even the Empire, newly minted as The First Order, seemed to have moved beyond the associations of racial purity from the original trilogy. After all, we had the presence of Finn as a storm trooper, and Crystal Clarke playing Ensign Goode on Starkiller Base. Beyond these two roles, however, we see little visibility for actors of color. We find them slightly more represented in the film as a whole doing voice work, or filling uncredited roles. A cursory glance through a complete cast listing on IMDb, for example, reveals a slightly increased presence of diversity, but nothing so substantial as to suggest a broader conscious attempt at inclusion.

Where *The Force Awakens* ultimately fails to move beyond the racialized history and memory of the franchise, though, is in how it crafts the evolution of Finn as a character. In the beginning, we see Finn clearly wrestling with the moral reality of what the First Order is doing. We watch as he is unable to bring himself to fire on innocent civilians during the raid on a Jakku village. We see him show compassion for a fallen comrade, even some shock and horror at the death and blood. We know that his emotional response to these events is so strong that it can be felt by Kylo Ren, who pauses to note the conflicted character. In later scenes, we witness his likeable conversations with Poe Dameron, a kind of comic bumbling as he attempts to escape by rescuing the captured pilot. After his forced return to Jakku, we see his earnest attempts at rescuing Rey from local thugs bent on capturing BB-8. All of this is meant to suggest a moral compass for the character, an emerging sense of self that resists the oppressive indoctrination of the First Order. It sets up an expectation that Finn will be a character to watch as he develops the strength to rise above his troubling beginnings and evolve into someone heroic. These seem like classical points for viewers to identify and be persuaded of Finn as a hero. This would be a classically structured monomyth if it were not for one troubling reality: Finn never actually achieves these goals.

As the narrative progresses, we see Finn reduced to these same characteristics in repeated fashion. All of his efforts to develop agency come with a kind of bumbling comedy. His attempts at convincing Rey that he is a part of the Resistance come with comic interplay between himself and BB-8. His attempts at convincing Han Solo that he is "kind of a big deal in the resistance" are rebuffed by the older character's casual admonishment that such lies are transparent. Later still, we see his honest nature come forward in an attempted rescue of Rey. Here also we see him largely reduced to comedic dialogue with Han Solo as he attempts to develop a plan. We also learn that his primary experience in serving Starkiller Base was that of a garbage man working in sanitation. All of this provides a troubling image of a character depicted as having heroic potential, but desperately limited in his ability to achieve those ends. His attempts and his dialogue are comical, and we laugh at him more than we laugh with him. While well-meaning and honestly intended, Finn is reduced to a level of caricature that, while not quite a Jar Jar Binks image of Steppin Fetchit/Zip Coon ante bellum minstrelsy shows, shares in a problematic racial and cultural memory of representation through similar character tropes.[11] Eric Lott's pivotal text *Love and Theft: Blackface Minstrelsy and the American Working Class*, explores how historical representations of race through blackface performance established a foundation point for popular culture ideas about Blackness and race.[12] These ideas, repeated and represented through the genre of science fiction, become a kind of "ethnoscape" that "provides a symbolic transfer of meaning between racial/ethnic politics and the shifting world of the sf text."[13] In effect, because our cultural narratives have not sufficiently resolved the racial tensions of our history and memory, we reenact these tensions in our science fiction narratives.

11. Taylor and Austin, *Darkest America*, 5.

12. Lott, *Love and Theft*, 93.

13. Lavender, *Race in American Science Fiction*. 158.

Nowhere is this clearer than in the final scenes of the film. Han Solo is dead, Chewbacca is nowhere to be found, and Rey appears to be unconscious. In a classical myth structure, this would be the moment for the hero character to rise to the occasion and demonstrate their emerging greatness. This would represent the test of their abilities and convictions. In the monomythic structure, so central to the *Star Wars* rhetoric, this is where Finn would overcome his great challenge, and emerge a hero. True to his moral compass, Finn will not shy from what is right, and engages the principal villain Kylo Ren. The encounter is comically one-sided. As Ren reduces Finn to a plaything, the latter ultimately succumbs to the assault and is rendered unconscious, only to be saved by Rey, now fully capable and invigorated by her latent Force abilities. The message is clear: the Force will not save the morally focused Black man, but if a young white woman is in trouble it will rise as needed. This final failure of Finn to be successful represents a trajectory of forced ineptitude for his character. At every turn, he attempts to act, only to have victory hinge on the efforts and luck of others. At no point in the narrative does the principal character of color succeed in developing or gaining any significant form of agency in the narrative except through the affordances of his white counterparts.[14] Finn is reduced to a supporting role, despite the visibility of his screen time and length of his dialogue. In effect, his characterization unmakes the very hope for something more racially equitable in the film universe by reinforcing the very memory and myth structure it attempts to resolve.

Star Wars, and The Old Republic

The failure of *The Force Awakens* is made doubly problematic by the fact that it fails to acknowledge a point that has long been accepted in *Star Wars* fandom, and through multiple iterations of what is now called the Expanded Universe. While these latter iterations are not considered canon, their presence and rhetorical impact provide a prescient model for what

14. It's worth noting that this article and argument were crafted long before the release of *The Last Jedi*. Rian Johnson's film is a good example of how to represent Finn in ways that don't rely on such overtly racist constructions, but instead offer a version of the character as an emerging hero learning his way. The jokes and experiences are not framed as laughter at Finn's expense, but as genuine opportunities for him to succeed and fail on his own merits. Indeed, there is a much larger argument to be made about how *The Last Jedi* is an articulate response to some of the critical narrative missteps of *The Force Awakens*.

Star Wars as a franchise might aspire to. The Expanded Universe works to follow a clear principle that "representation matters."

Of note in the Expanded Universe is the role of games that allow players to immerse themselves in the narrative framework of *Star Wars*. While *Star Wars* games have been around for many years (the first iteration was the 1983 Atari arcade console featuring the assault on the Death Star), most games focused on players controlling principal characters from the existing franchise. Other games, generally classed as flight simulators, allowed players to control unnamed and unviewed characters as pilots in the galactic conflict.[15] In the genre of first-person shooters players were allowed to assume the identity of Kyle Katarn,[16] a character later expanded in various novels and graphic novels. In each of these games, though, player identity is largely determined, and what racial visibility exists, is largely coded as White.

With the arrival of *Knights of the Old Republic* in 2003, Bioware became one of the first publicly visible game developers to actively begin to advocate for diverse representations in games, in terms of race, gender, and sexuality. Their efforts particularly matter for this argument because of how the rhetorical choices of characterization produce affordances for player identification. Bioware is largely recognized for making role-playing games with multiple franchises like *Mass Effect*, *Dragon Age*, and *The Old Republic* (which includes both the single-player games *Knights of the Old Republic I* and *II*, as well as the MMOG *The Old Republic*, which share a narrative universe). The principal game designers for these franchises have long been invested in creating diverse characters in their games, while making those inclusions feel both organic and significant. Characters of diverse races and sexualities are not "token" appearances, but rather serve as a significant and compelling narrative focus of the experience.[17]

15. See the *X-Wing/Tie Fighter* series by Totally Games for more examples of this.

16. See the *Dark Forces* series by Raven Software for further examples of this.

17. Grayson, "Bioware's Heir."

An image from *Star Wars: The Old Republic*, a game that allows
players to adjust avatars through a variety of sliders.

In each of Bioware's *Star Wars* iterations, players can create diverse hero
characters by defining through the interface the racial and physical dynamics of the player avatar. In addition, the supporting cast of party members reflect this commitment to diversity. There are always characters of
diverse races, species, and sexuality that are well-rounded and dynamic;
their character evolution is a part of the story that we play. The cast of
non-player characters with whom a party might interact equally capture
what a truly diverse galaxy might look like. This image is even more compelling because the presence of such galactic diversity is so well-saturated
that it does not draw attention to itself. It simply appears as normal. The
normalization of diversity in a *Star Wars* narrative that relies on the rhetorical markers of myth-making means that the narrative itself operates
as a persuasive text, producing hero figures that embody, represent, and
signify all the positive attributes of a diverse social system. In effect, we
don't need an external argument about the need for diversity, we simply
see and experience that it works.

It's important to note the function of the digital role-playing game
here, as the characteristics of that artifact help shape the level of interactiv-
ity necessary to produce generative player response. Digital role-playing
games are about creating and controlling characters through a combina-
tion of game mechanics and narrative affordances that allow players to
immerse themselves in an experience.[18] Such levels of immersion allow

18. Call et al., "From Dungeons to Digital Denizens," 17.

players to create a memory specific to their own choices and agency. Through deciding how a character looks, in addition to how a character is perceived and seen by other players, a new rhetorical argument emerges that is highly persuasive specifically because it has been narrowly crafted for the specific identification of the player. The narrative of *Star Wars* ceases to be about the degree to which participants can "see" themselves in a character, but instead becomes a matter of the degree to which a player can create, define, and perform as a character. In effect, players are not being persuaded by an external image, but instead co-creating a played-story experience in the *Star Wars* universe. They create a rhetoric of identification from within the player that is further reinforced by continued experience in the game world. It is a subtle shift from viewers to players, but it suggests a degree of agency that is essential for making not only memory, but a living mythology of the experience. To wit, the act of making decisions about a character's identity coupled with what a character does, generates myth by creating identifiable memories within the thematic and narrative context of the *Star Wars* universe. It allows players to see themselves and others in inclusive and diverse ways.

Conclusions

Star Wars has a fraught history. From Lando to Jar Jar and beyond, the narrative arc of the *Star Wars* universe has been a shifting tide of complicated racial constructions and representations. The flagship films of the franchise, though, have been the primary sources of this tension. The troubling trend of tokenizing diversity has yet to be resolved in any meaningful way, and the films' inability to adequately move beyond their own racial limitations is overshadowed by the overwhelming success of other franchise elements. Even the most recent media additions 2016's *Rogue One*, 2017's *The Last Jedi*, and the now-canonical *Star Wars Rebels* serial include greater and more persuasive representations of diversity than the principal films have been able to provide. Fans and Internet readers everywhere are now likely familiar with the "representation matters" conversation regarding the presence of Diego Luna in *Rogue One*, and the impact of his visibility for viewers.[19] Still, when considering the role of *Star Wars* in creating a myth-like experience for fans and viewers, many of the primary films continue to fall short of what more creative iterations accomplish. More to the point,

19. Tejada, "Rogue One."

the films continue to propagate a rhetorical myth structure that is rooted in failed or shortsighted attempts. Where the games and other *Star Wars* stories succeed brilliantly, *The Force Awakens* continues a trend of abject tokenization. Those responsible for this film refuse to countenance the possibility of what an authentically diverse cast might provide for the story, and the rhetorical implications that might afford the audience. As any *Star Wars* fan knows, the absence of belief will always lead to failure.

Bibliography

Bioware. *Star Wars: Knights of the Old Republic*. Edmonton, 2003.

Brooker, Will. "Reading of Racism: Interpretation, Stereotyping and *The Phantom Menace*." *Continuum: Journal of Media and Cultural Studies* 15:1 (2001) 15–32. http://www.tandfonline.com/doi/abs/10.1080/713657758.

Burke, Kenneth. *A Rhetoric of Motives*. Berkeley, CA: University of California Press, 1969.

Call, Joshua, et al. "From Dungeons to Digital Denizens." In *Dungeons, Dragons, and Digital Denizens: The Digital Role Playing Game*, edited by Gerald A. Voorhees, et al., 11–24. New York: Bloomsbury, 2012.

Campbell, Joseph. *The Hero with a Thousand Faces*. Novato, CA: New World Library, 2008.

Gordon, Andrew. "*Star Wars*: A Myth for Our Time." In *Screening the Sacred: Religion, Myth, and Ideology in Popular American Film*, edited by Joel W. Martin and Conrad E. Ostwalt, 73–82. Boulder, CO: Westview, 1995. Originally published in *Literature/ Film Quarterly* 6:4 (Fall 1978) 314–26.

Grayson, Nathan. "Bioware's Heir on Sexism, Racism, Homophobia in Games." *Rock Paper Shotgun*, March 27, 2014. https://www.rockpapershotgun.com/2014/03/27/manveer-heir-interview.

Lavender, Isiah. *Race in American Science Fiction*. Bloomington, IN: Indiana University Press, 2011.

Lee, Benjamin. "Twitter Trolls Urge Boycott of Star Wars Over Black Character." *The Guardian*. October 20, 2015. https://www.theguardian.com/film/2015/oct/20/twitter-trolls-boycott-star-wars-black-character-force-awakens-john-boyega.

Lott, Eric. *Love and Theft: Blackface, Minstrelsy, and the American Working Class*. New York: Oxford University Press, 2013.

Lyden, John C. "The Apocalyptic Cosmology of Star Wars." *Journal of Religion & Film* 4:1 (2000). http://digitalcommons.unomaha.edu/jrf/vol4/iss1/2.

Nama, Adilifu. *Black Space: Imagining Race in Science Fiction Film*. Austin, TX: University of Texas Press, 2008.

Parry, Baillie. "Kelly Marie Tran is Dealing with Horrifying Racist and Sexist Comments Following 'Last Jedi.'" *pizzabottle*. January 1, 2018. https://pizzabottle.com/69174-kelly-marie-tran-is-dealing-with-racist-and-sexist-comments-following-last-jedi.

Peters, Timothy. "The Force as Law: Mythology, Ideology, and Order in George Lucas' *Star Wars*." *Australian Feminist Law Journal* 36:1 (2012) 125–43.

Renshaw, David. "John Boyega." *V Magazine*, October 7, 2015. http://vman.com/article/john-boyega.

Taylor, Yuval, and Jake Austen. *Darkest America: Black Minstrelsy from Slavery to Hip-Hop*. New York: W. W. Norton, 2012.

Tejada, Chloe. "'Rogue One' Fan Reminds Us Why 'Representation Matters.'" *The Huffington Post Canada*, January 5, 2017. http://www.huffingtonpost.ca/2017/01/05/rogue-one-representation_n_13973296.html.

Thrasher, Steven. "Star Wars: A Salute to Black Stormtroopers." *The Guardian*, December 29, 2014. https://www.theguardian.com/film/filmblog/2014/dec/29/star-wars-force-awakens-black-stormtrooper.

CHAPTER 7

RITUAL, REPETITION, AND THE RESPONSIBILITY OF RELAYING THE MYTH

JUSTIN MULLIS

Abstract: This essay charts the history of *Star Wars* fans' tumultuous relationship with franchise creator George Lucas. Drawing on the theories and insights of writers and scholars such as Bruce Lincoln, John C. Lyden, Andrew Briton, Hiroki Azuma, Jonathan Z. Smith, Tom Shone, and Ben Brazil, the argument is made that the relationship between Lucas and his fans can be understood as comparable to that of the relationship that exists between a hierophant and their devotees in a traditional religious setting. However, Lucas's subsequent decision to tamper with the sacred canon of *Star Wars* with the Special Editions re-releases, and his altering of core elements of *Star Wars* mythology via the poorly received Prequel Trilogy, made Lucas guilty of sacrilege, leading to his eventual rejection by *Star Wars* fans. This rejection in turn opened up a position of power that would eventually be filled by J. J. Abrams, whose film successfully returned the saga to a more conservative status quo.

Introduction

One of the most striking aspects of 2015's *Star Wars Episode VII: The Force Awakens* is that it is, in many ways, identical to the original *Star Wars*—otherwise known as *Star Wars Episode IV: A New Hope*—released in theaters in 1977, with some even calling *The Force Awakens* a virtual re-make of the now classic film.[1] These similarities have prompted many com-mentators to ask why a film so clearly derivative would be so well received by so many, as the movie was not only a box office hit, becoming one of the most successful films of all time, but was also greeted by an overwhelm-ingly positive reception by the franchise's many ardent fans. To answer this question I will turn not to the film itself but rather to those who made it such a success: the fans.

As film critic David Edelstein observed in his review of *The Force Awakens*, much of the film's success had do with fans' feelings that director J. J. Abrams—also a self-professed fan of *Star Wars*—was more faithful to the fandom's collective vision of the *Star Wars* universe than George Lucas, the man who had created it. Edelstein writes:

> I often think back to 2003, when [I attended] a *Lord of the Rings* movie marathon . . . A young woman I interviewed actually teared up explaining that *Rings* director Peter Jackson did a great job because he was a *fan* of Tolkien's books and understood what they meant to other fans. Against this, she cited Lucas's *Star Wars* prequels, which made billions but left most people cold (except for Jar Jar, who left them livid). Lucas *created Star Wars*, she said, but because he wasn't a *fan* he forgot why people responded to the first film. That a sequel made by a fan would be better than one by a creator [once] seemed counter intuitive . . . but as fan culture has become more dominant (and lucrative), the idea now seems prescient. [It was] the subtext of Lucas's words at a recent Kennedy Center event, where he said—with a touch of sadness—that *The Force Awakens* was the *Star Wars* movie the fans have been looking for and that (by implication) he didn't give them.[2]

Following Edelstein, I will argue that the resounding success of *The Force Awakens* can be attributed in large part to the removal of Lucas from the creative process by Disney and his replacement with fan-cum-director Abrams. Not because Abrams is a better director than Lucas *per se*, but because for many of *Star Wars'* most faithful fans Lucas had erred in his decisions to follow after his own artistic impulses in updating the *Star Wars* franchise via the 1997 Special Edition re-edits of the Original Trilogy

1. See Sullivan's "Star Wars" for a list of eighteen ways in which the plots of *The Force Awakens* and *Star Wars* (1977) align. See Anderton's "VOTD" for a video version of the same argument.

2. Edelstein, "The Force Awakens."

(1977–1983) of *Star Wars* films and then compounded these transgressions by subsequently releasing the highly revisionist Prequel Trilogy between 1999 and 2005. Despite the fact that such alterations and additions were met with vocal objections by his congregation, Lucas persisted in continually revising the *Star Wars* canon until he eventually sold the franchise to Disney in October of 2012, a decision that seems largely motivated by Lucas's own openly melancholy if not outright hostile disposition regarding his fan's desire for things to simply stay the same.

Definitions

Before proceeding any further, I want to be clear what I mean when speaking about "fans." In our modern media-saturated culture, many people claim to be "fans" of many different things, making it appear as if the term *fan* is merely shorthand for "liking" something, a fact that has resulted in some commentators calling into question the utility of the label altogether along with the larger constructs of "fandoms" or "fan cultures."[3]

Moving away from such generalized notions of "fans" and "fandoms," we turn to the ethnographic work of sociologist Yoshimasa Kijima, whose study of Japanese video game fans defines such fans, known as "gamers," as individuals who play video games "masochistically," i.e., deriving maximum pleasure by making what should be a leisure activity actively unpleasant. Gamers do this, Kijima explains, by engaging in "self-punishing and exhaustive game play," grueling practices that would undoubtedly take the fun out of gaming for more "casual" video game players, but which actually enhances the pleasure experienced by seasoned gamers.[4]

Like video games and other popular forms of entertainment media, Hollywood movies are also generally seen as a leisure activity. Theoretical

3. This has been especially apparent with regards to sociologist Yoshimasa Kijima's principal subject of study, "Gamers," who are discussed in more detail in the following paragraph. However, in late 2014 video game columnist Leigh Alexander penned the divisive editorial "'Gamers' Don't Have to Be Your Audience. 'Gamers' Are Over," in which she argued that the ubiquity of video games as a means of entertainment meant that the specialized designation of "Gamer" no longer made sense and should be abandoned by the video game industry. Alexander's piece resulted in a wave of subsequent pieces on the same topic from additional video game columnists and was eventually picked up by mainstream newsgroups like *The Daily Beast* and *The Guardian*, all of whom echoed her general sentiment.

4. Kijima, "The Fighting Game," 252.

film critic Andrew Britton writes that "entertainment . . . defines itself in opposition to labor, or, more generally, to the large category 'the rest of life.'" The central promise of entertainment, Britton argues, is to provide us with an escape from the drudgery and stress of mundane existence. Entertainment "tells us that we are 'off duty' and that nothing is required of us but to sit back, relax, and enjoy."[5] This promise simultaneously makes entertainment highly gratifying and highly trivial.

However, fans do not see entertainment in the same way as other consumers. Rather than an indication that they are intellectually and creatively "off duty," fans see such media as fuel for their own personal cerebral and artistic forges. As demonstrated by Henry Jenkins in his landmark work *Textual Poachers*, rather than being passive consumers of popular-culture, fans use "the semiotic raw material [that] media provides" to construct imagined worlds that they inhabit, an idea that I will be returning to shortly.[6]

In following Kijima's line of argumentation, in conjunction with the additional insights of Britton and Jenkins, I propose broadening Kijima's definition of "fan" to encompass not just video game fans but all fans, thereby redefining the term as one that designates those individuals who not only consume media but are actively and willingly consumed by it in turn and who find such mutual consumption to be extremely meaningful.

In addition it is also worth reminding readers of scholar Victoria Nelson's observation that the term *fan*, "short form of *fanatic*," was originally a piece of religious nomenclature being derived from "the Latin *fanaticus* (lit. "temple attendant," from *fanus*, "temple") [and] denoting someone exhibiting an overzealous sense of religious devotion."[7] According to Nelson, "the first modern nonreligious usage of the short form fan" appeared "in U.S. newspapers [in] the late nineteenth century in reference to sports devotees" and later was "stretched to include ardent enthusiasts of the new mass entertainment genres of movies and science fiction, fantasy, and horror literature."[8] Considering such an etymology, one can potentially see this essay as part of a larger move to revisit the original religious meaning of the term "fan" in order to see how the academic discipline of Religious Studies might help to better understand the phenomena that are modern fandoms.

---

5. Britton, "Blissing Out," 100–1.
6. Jenkins, *Textual Poachers*, 49.
7. Nelson, *Gothicka*, 51.
8. Ibid.

In my prior work[9] I have argued that fans, as previously defined, should be understood as individuals engaged in "recreational religious activity" (to borrow a phrase from scholar Robert M. Price),[10] in which such individuals form communities around imaginative pop-culture texts like *Star Wars*. These texts allow fans to construct what ritual theorist Adam B. Seligman calls "subjunctive 'as-if' worlds"[11] that serve as a means of acting out a desired reality, one which does not objectively exist but which is understood to be preferable to the one which does. This process is analogous to that described by Jonathan Z. Smith in his famous essay "The Bare Facts of Ritual." For Smith the conjunction of myths and rituals provide their practitioners with a direct line to the subjunctive, thereby alleviating existential tension that occurs naturally as the byproduct of living in a seemingly unordered and confusing world.[12]

Evidence of this process can be seen in journalist Ethan Gilsdorf's semi-autobiographical exploration of fantasy fandom, *Fantasy Freaks and Gaming Geeks*, in which he relates how as a preteen he came to "believe" in the fantasy and sci-fi worlds he encountered in pop culture in contrast to those of traditional religion: "I didn't believe in God, or in heaven and hell. But Middle-earth's lands, or a D&D labyrinth, or a science fiction universe like *Star Wars*—those were places I could believe in, and visit as often as I liked."[13]

Gilsdorf's testimony, in which he confesses to finding traditional religious ideas like God and an afterlife too inaccessible and unconvincing to be comforting, in contrast to the "subjunctive 'as-if' worlds" of popular-culture, "like *Star Wars*," also brings to light what historian Michael Saler contends is arguably the biggest advantage which modern fandoms present over traditional religion. Fandoms, rather than asking their devotees to repudiate the empirical world around them in favor of concepts that lack strong empirical evidence but which they find existentially comforting, only ask their adherents to, in the words of writer Mark Dery, "believ[e] as-if rather than believing in" the myths they preach.[14] For this reason Saler, taking after German sociologist Max Weber, contends that in this

9. Mullis, "Playing Games."

10. Price, Foreword, 165.

11. Seligman et al., *Ritual and its Consequences*, 103.

12. Smith, "The Bare Facts," 56–65.

13. Gilsdorf, *Fantasy Freaks*, 10–11.

14. Dery, "Kraken Rising."

modern age of "disenchantment," when religious sources of meaning and inspiration are considered highly suspect, fandoms have risen up as traditional religions' fiercest and most successful competitor.[15]

It is my contention then that it is only by understanding fan cultures as a type of religious expression that we can best make sense out of the many actions, obsessions, and outrageous behaviors that so often befuddle outside observers when looking in on the world of fandom. This includes, but is by no means limited to, the reason why films like *The Force Awakens* are often so well received by fans despite their many obvious shortcomings in terms of originality. It will also help to account for the often contentious relationship that has long existed between fans of *Star Wars* and the franchise's creator George Lucas.

Theory and Methods

The tendency of fans to butt heads with the creators, or more often today the corporate proprietors, of the fictive universes they love is as old as the modern institution of fandom itself. Saler writes that the earliest of all modern fandoms may very well be that of Sherlock Holmes, whose fans are known as Sherlockians, and who can also claim to have started the oldest and longest lasting fan club, The Baker Street Irregulars, founded in 1934. While the early Sherlockians were often the butt of many jokes in both the UK and US press, two individuals who found their antics particularly displeasing were Denis and Adrian Doyle, sons of Holmes creator Sir Arthur Conan Doyle, and trustees of the Conan Doyle Estate. After attending a Baker Street Irregulars gala and learning that these fans were more enamored with their father's creation then Doyle himself, both sons began sending frequent letters to the Irregulars ordering them to "Cease, Desist and Disband."[16] While the example of the Sherlockians is one in which a creator, or in this case his representatives, demonstrated hostility towards their fandom, the flip-side of this relationship, in which fans display hostility towards a creator, should also be noted as both are apparent in the case of George Lucas and *Star Wars* fandom. A classic example of the latter is the 1996 outcry by Japanese fans of the wildly popular anime show *Neon Genesis Evangelion* (1995/96), who found themselves so incensed by the series' admittedly nonsensical finale that Gainax Studios, where the

15. Saler, *As If*, 164.
16. Ibid., 121.

show was produced, was vandalized while series creator Hideaki Anno was sent death threats via email.[17] With regards to *Star Wars* fandom the best example of the often contentious relationship that can exist between fans and a creator is the continual debate as to whether or not Lucas violated the sacredness of the *Star Wars* canon via his continual "updating" and "revising" of the Original Trilogy of films in an effort to try to fulfill his own artistic perfectionist impulses.

To help make sense of this controversy, I turn to historian of religion Bruce Lincoln's 1996 essay "Mythic Narrative and Cultural Diversity in American Society," which addresses the contentious rapport often found between those whose job it is to narrate myths and those whose job it is to listen. Regarding how myth functions in society, Lincoln refers back to historian Paul Veyne's formulation that "the essence of myth is not that everyone knows it but that it is supposed to be known and is worthy of being known by all."[18] This definition, while perhaps not the most particular, works very well in making sense of how fans treat pop culture products in a fashion identical to traditional myths. It is not that everyone knows the traditional myths of their religion or culture or that everyone has seen acclaimed films like *Star Wars*. But for devotees of a given myth cycle or fans of a particular piece of pop-culture, the central belief is that everyone should know these stories, that they are "worthy of being known," and that knowing them will somehow change the life of the hearer or viewer for the better. This formulation of what myths are and how they operate leads Lincoln to state that there are always two groups of people who are guaranteed to get the most out of a myth: "Those who tell such stories most often and those who are most fully captivated by them."[19] In a traditional religious context these two roles would usually be occupied by the hierophant, as storyteller, and the devotees, as listeners. In the context of fandom these two roles can be understood as belonging to the creator and fans.

This point about who is most invested in myths leads directly into Lincoln's analysis of the tension that he sees as arising between "those who know the story well," i.e., the devotees or fans, and the "narrator whose version compares unfavorably with others they have heard or one who introduces too many novelties into a story."[20] Lincoln sees this tense

17. Cavallaro, *The Art*, 59 and 104.
18. Lincoln, "Mythic Narrative," 175.
19. Ibid., 166.
20. Ibid., 167.

relationship as part of an organic system of checks and balances, which assures that a given story is told and continues to be told in a way that is deemed acceptable by those who have invested the myth with so much importance in their lives.

Case Study

Though some *Star Wars* fans have always taken issue with a few of Lucas's creative decisions on the Original Trilogy—the most well-known example being the presence of the teddy bear-like Ewoks in 1983's *Return of the Jedi*[21]—the real trouble began in the late 1990s, when Lucas decided to retroactively alter the Original Trilogy via the removal and insertion of various visual and narrative elements. These New Revised Standard Versions of the original three *Star Wars* films are what would come to be known as the Special Edition versions and were each released in theaters during the first three months of 1997. The multiple alterations that Lucas made to the Original Trilogy and the subsequent fan backlash to them has been well documented, with two notable sources being the 2010 documentary *The People vs. George Lucas* (Dir. Alexandre O. Philippe), and film and religion scholar John C. Lyden's 2012 essay "Whose Film Is It, Anyway? Canonicity and Authority in *Star Wars* Fandom."[22]

One of the best-known alterations deals with the fatal encounter between smuggler Han Solo and the alien bounty hunter Greedo in the Mos Eisley cantina in *Star Wars*. In the original 1977 cut of the film Han Solo is confronted by Greedo, who points a gun at Han at nearly point-blank range. Han, being a quick talker, manages to distract Greedo long enough to slip his blaster out of his holster and fire under the table, killing Greedo before the alien can get off a single shot. The 1997 Special Edition version alters this scene by making it appear as if Greedo shoots first. Because it seems unimaginable that a seasoned bounty hunter would fail to hit a target sitting less than three feet in front of him, Han's head and neck were digitally manipulated to make it look as if Han somehow dodges the laser blast (!) before returning

---

21. For a discussion of *Star Wars* fans' dislike of the Ewoks see Scalzi, *The Rough Guide*, 122. However it should be clarified that, as writer Caroline Siede notes, *Star Wars* fans' dislike of the Ewoks rarely indicates a dislike for the film they are in, a fact that distinguishes such earlier manifestations of fan discontent with later post-1990s manifestations. Siede, "If You like."

22. Lyden, "Whose Film."

fire, this time above the table. The altered scene is comical to say the least, and so in 2004 Lucas altered the film again, this time for the Original Trilogy's inaugural DVD release, making it now appear as if both Han and Greedo fire simultaneously, with Greedo still somehow missing, while Han's head jerk to the side has been significantly minimized. Evidently still not happy, Lucas altered the scene once again for the 2011 Blu-ray release, this time shortening the scene by removing several frames, perhaps in order to make the visual discrepancies created by his prior alterations less apparent.

In the original 1977 cut of **Star Wars**, Han removes his blaster and fires a single shot under the table resulting in a white flash and puff of smoke. In the next shot Greedo lies dead on the table without having fired a single shot.

In the 1997 Special Edition re-edit of **Star Wars**, Greedo fires a red laser blast at Han whose head unnaturally jerks out of the way as the smuggler returns fire above the table with his own red laser blast.

Lyden writes that all such changes were seen by many fans as a betrayal of the relationship described by Lincoln, a violation of the sacred canon of *Star Wars*, an act which, in a traditional religious context, would be seen as tantamount to heresy if not outright sacrilege. This alteration spawned what has come to be known as the "Han Shot First" controversy in which fans, upset over a change that they argue retroactively alters Han Solo's personality and weakens his overall character arc of heartless rogue to selfless hero of the Rebellion, protested via the launching of petitions, websites, the creation of t-shirts, and other similar demonstrations.[23]

In 2012 Lucas responded to the "Han Shot First" controversy, saying:

> Well, it's not a religious event. I hate to tell people that. It's a movie, just a movie. The controversy over who shot first, Greedo or Han Solo . . . what I did was try to clean up the confusion, but obviously it upset people because they wanted Solo to be a cold-blooded killer, but he actually isn't.[24]

As Lyden notes, "Lucas defends the change [by denying] that there was any change" despite evidence to the contrary, and by claiming that all his revisions did was make "what 'really' happened" more apparent.[25] But Lucas also contradicts himself by first denying the significance of his alterations by attempting to emphasize the trivialness of the product—"It's a movie, just a movie"—in contrast to a "religious event"; a parallel which seems to indicate that Lucas is fully aware of how many fans view his *Star Wars* films. It should also be pointed out that Lucas—or more likely someone writing copy for him—has, on at least one occasion, also openly acknowledged that Han shot first in a May 2006 post on the official *Star Wars* website announcing the forthcoming release of the unaltered versions of the original films on DVD, which will be discussed in more detail later.[26] Ultimately Lucas's rhetorical strategies for justifying the alteration of an iconic scene from the original 1977 film amounts to what psychoanalyst Tamaki Saitō would call a classic example of using disavowal to acknowledge something by denying it.[27]

---

23. From a purely academic standpoint I side with those who argue that Han did shoot first. The best evidence for this view so far is a copy of a 1976 fourth edition shooting-script discovered in the archives of the University of New Brunswick library by Kristian Brown. Though the script is very early—Luke Skywalker is still referred to by his original name, Luke Starkiller, for example—it nevertheless demonstrates that the confrontation between Han and Greedo was originally envisioned with Han being the only person to fire a shot. See Bingley, "Copy of Original Star Wars Script."

24. Block, "5 Questions with George Lucas."

25. Lyden, "Whose Film," 778.

26. "This September."

27. Saitō, *Beautiful Fighting Girl*, 83.

George Lucas photographed on the set of *Indiana Jones and the Kingdom of the Crystal Skull* (2008) wearing a fan-made "Han Shot First" t-shirt. Chris Taylor, author of *How Star Wars Conquered the Universe*, has interpreted Lucas's fashion choice as an attempt to "stoke" the fires of controversy surrounding his alteration of this iconic scene in the 1977 film.[28]

The fact that Lucas defended the Special Edition as a better representation of his artistic vision of the Original Trilogy and argued that it was his prerogative as the creator of the *Star Wars* franchise to see that vision

28. "George Lucas Knows."

through, even if that vision was something that nobody else cared for, was interestingly even made into a selling point by producer Rick McCallum, who, at a 2001 press conference for the soon to be released Special Edition DVDs, said:

> And one of the great things about doing the Special Editions was we were able to go back and do the original *Star Wars: A New Hope* exactly the way George wanted it. The way he had written it. Whether people liked it, it didn't matter, it was his movie and he couldn't make it when he first made it because there were so many compromises he had to go through.[29]

Whether this line of argumentation actually helped Lucasfilm sell more DVDs is unclear, but it certainly marks what may be one of the only times in history that a producer has openly told consumers that they are actively in the business of selling them a product without concern over whether they like it or not.

Such offenses were subsequently compounded by Lucas's production of the Prequel Trilogy of *Star Wars* films, which continued to deviate significantly from both the visual and narrative style of the Original Trilogy. Lucas replaced the practical special effects of the Original Trilogy with computer generated imagery, for example, and shifted the tone from a rousing space opera to one of a political/military drama. The Prequel Trilogy also further altered the established canon of *Star Wars* mythology via such innovations as the introduction of midi-chlorians as a naturalized explanation for the previously mystical powers of The Force. Lucas knew that such changes would be unpopular, saying, "I knew . . . I was doing exactly what the fans didn't want me to do . . . [I was] doing things that were very uncommercial with a very commercial property."[30] True enough, many *Star Wars* fans found the introduction of such novelties into a myth they knew so well both unwelcome and offensive, leading many of them to act out against and subsequently reject Lucas's role as pontiff of the *Star Wars* universe.[31] In addition, Lucas also left no one but himself to blame for these deviations. Unlike the Original Trilogy for which Lucas was only responsible for writing and directing the first installment, Lucas pulled solo duty on all three of the Prequel films. Despite its rightful claim as a classic of the genre, 1977's *Star Wars* is, as science fiction author and film historian John Scalzi writes, nonetheless

29. "Q & A with Van Ling."
30. Shone, *Blockbuster*, 288.
31. Lyden, "Whose Film," 780.

a "dry and unpalatable" movie only made serviceable by its groundbreaking special effects.[32] Lucas made the right decision back in 1980 and 1983 to hand the reins over to more seasoned directors and writers for the Original Trilogy's second and third installments.

All this, however, is not to say that the Prequels were not financially successful. Like *The Force Awakens*, 1999's *The Phantom Menace* was the highest grossing film of its year, netting a worldwide box office of $923.1 million.[33] Nevertheless, as film critic Tom Shone demonstrates in his illuminating history of the summer blockbuster, a strong box office is really no indication that a particular film is popular, only that its marketers have done a good job of selling it. The *Star Wars* Prequels, Shone writes, are a textbook example of this[34] as the movies' box office takes were undoubtedly helped not only by multiple lucrative marketing deals signed by Lucasfilm, what Shone calls a "promotional black hole"[35] that sucked in nearly every major advertiser, but also by the fact that *Star Wars* fans committed themselves to watching the films multiple times in theaters; not because they enjoyed them but because they hoped that repeat exposure would make them eventually like the movies—an idea that recalls Kojima's contention regarding the masochistic behavior of fans.[36] However, the real unpopularity of the Prequels can be gauged by the fact that when Lucas re-released *The Phantom Menace* in 3D in theaters in 2012 the film tanked. Fans, as well as general audiences, might have been willing to see the Prequels multiple times upon their original release but few were willing to pay to see them again, unlike the Special Edition versions of the Original Trilogy when re-released in 1997.[37]

32. Scalzi, *The Rough Guide*, 119.

33. Shone, *Blockbuster*, 292.

34. See page 15 of *Blockbuster* for Shone's discussion of several films which grossed $200–300+ million at the box office but which nobody liked. See pages 272–73 for Shone's discussion of films that are remembered as box office flops due to their unpopularity but which actually performed very well. Finally, see page 288 for Shone's declaration that, with regard to the *Star Wars* Prequels, "the box office tells you nothing" concerning how popular the films actually were.

35. Shone, *Blockbuster*, 276.

36. Shone, *Blockbuster*, 284. Shone further documents *Star Wars* fans' commitment to their franchise on page 276, noting that when 20th Century Fox premiered the teaser trailer for *The Phantom Menace* in front of the film *The Siege* that movie's box office jumped an astounding 85 percent above what was anticipated, as numerous *Star Wars* lovers paid full price to see the trailer and then promptly left the theater.

37. Smith, "'Star Wars." Lucas had initially planned to re-release all three Star Wars

The unfavorable release of the Special Edition versions of the Original Trilogy and the unpopular Prequel Trilogy a few years later resulted in schisms within the *Star Wars* fandom. Certain factions of fans, whom I will be calling Original Trilogy Exclusivists, denounced the Prequels insisting that there were only three *Star Wars* movies—the Original Trilogy—while an even more vocal subset, whom I call Original Trilogy Purists, condemned Lucas for the alterations made to the Original Trilogy and petitioned the director to release the unaltered versions of the original films.[38] Initially Lucas responded to such petitions by refusing to release the unaltered version of the Original Trilogy, only making the Special Edition available on DVD in 2004. In an interview from that same year Lucas told fans that he was

> sorry you saw half a completed film and fell in love with it. But I want it to be the way I want it to be. I'm the one who has to take responsibility for it. I'm the one who has to have everybody throw rocks at me all the time, so at least if they're going to throw rocks at me, they're going to throw rocks at me for something I love rather than something I think is not very good, or at least something I think is not finished.[39]

Lucas's tone here—which could be seen as fluctuating between that of a condescending parent ("I'm sorry . . ."), a self-righteous St. Stephen ("I'm the one who has to have everybody throw rocks at me all the time"), and a child throwing a tantrum ("I want it to be the way I want it to be")—speaks to the growing rift between Lucas as hierophant and his increasingly uneasy congregation of fans.

In 2006 Lucas finally acquiesced and had the Original Trilogy released as part of a new DVD box set alongside the Special Editions. These releases however turned out to be extremely poor, being sourced from a 1993 laserdisc release without even being subject to the most basic touchup or restoration work—the films were not even presented in an anamorphic format, meaning they wouldn't show up properly if viewed on a modern widescreen television. In an interview with MTV about the release, Lucas is described

---

Prequel films in 2012. However the poor box-office performance of *The Phantom Menace* resulted in a cancellation of those plans. Eight months after the re-release of *The Phantom Menace* tanked Lucasfilm was sold to Walt Disney Studios.

38. I am indebted to Andy Kluthe and Andrew Bridgman's comic "The 8 Types of Star Wars Fans" for the categories "Original Trilogy Exclusivists" and "Original Trilogy Purists."

39. "Lucas Talks."

as attempting to bait his fans and is quoted mockingly remarking that "now we'll find out whether they [the fans] *really* wanted the originals or whether they want the improved versions. It'll all come out in the end."[40] In reaction, fans assigned these versions of the Original Trilogy the insulting moniker of GOUT for George's Original Unaltered Theatrical versions.[41]

Lucas further responded to this criticism by stating that he was not interested in allocating the necessary time or money needed to restore the theatrical versions of the Original Trilogy and that as far as he was concerned those versions "didn't even exist anymore."[42] This was a view that Lucas made even more explicit when he refused to give the National Film Registry a copy of the original unaltered 1977 version of *Star Wars*, even though the Library of Congress has one.[43] Many fans derided Lucas as a hypocrite for this stance, citing a 1988 speech Lucas once delivered to the assembled US Congress in which he asserted that "People who alter or destroy works of art and our cultural heritage for profit or as an exercise of power are barbarians," and that if such practices were allowed to continue that in the future "many [film] archivists [will] have . . . to go to Eastern bloc countries where American films have been better preserved."[44]

One of the many ironies in Lucas's statement about film preservation is that some *Star Wars* fans have banded together and engaged in various industrious, though often illegal, attempts to reclaim the Original Trilogy as it existed prior to Lucas's tampering. These fans have done this via amateur film restoration efforts that they have subsequently made available online. The most well-known example is the Despecialized Edition created by Czechoslovakian *Star Wars* fan Petr Harmáček, who goes by the alias

40. Vineyard, "George Lucas."

41. "Got GOUT?"

42. "Lucas Talks."

43. Eveleth, "The *Star Wars*."

44. Lussier, "George Lucas." Lucas's full remarks on the issue read: "and if the laws of the United States continue to condone this behavior, history will surely classify us as a barbaric society. Today, engineers with their computers can add color to black-and-white movies, change the soundtrack, speed up the pace, and add or subtract material to the philosophical tastes of the copyright holder. Tomorrow, more advanced technology will be able to replace actors with 'fresher faces,' or alter dialogue and change the movement of the actor's lips to match. It will soon be possible to create a new 'original' negative with whatever changes or alterations the copyright holder of the moment desires. The copyright holders, so far, have not been completely diligent in preserving the original negatives of films they control." Again Lucas's remarks are ironic as he is responsible for doing *all* of these things to the Original Trilogy.

"Harmy" online.[45] Described as a "guerilla restorationist" by Radio Prague, Harmáček's actions have been compared to that of previous generations of "young Czechs [who] opposed . . . the communist regime's re-writing of history" by "smuggling . . . books and other materials" out of the country; an analogy that conversely also paints Lucas as an autocrat engaged in acts of "Orwellian petulance."[46] However Harmáček's activities might also be compared to those of a religious reformation leader who seeks to restore sacred Scripture to its original form and distribute it amongst the common people despite opposition from clerical authorities.

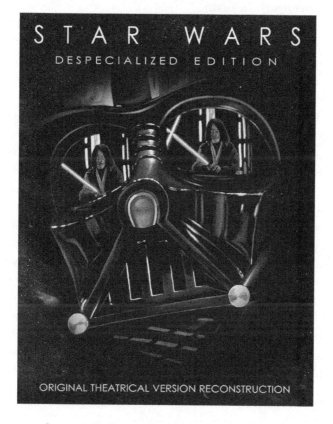

Poster created by Christian Waggoner for the Despecialized Edition
of the Original Trilogy, a fan-restoration by Petr "Harmy" Harmáček.

45. Hosie, "'Star Wars: Despecialized Edition.'" Readers are strongly encouraged to watch "Harmy's Star Wars" (posted online by HanDuet), a video created by Harmáček that explains both his philosophical reasons for, as well as the technical aspects of, his restoration of the Original Trilogy.

46. Jůn, "The Czech Guerilla Restorationist."

Of course, the principal concern for fans like Harmáček is not being branded an iconoclast but being sued for copyright infringement. However, when asked in a 2014 interview with *The Atlantic* about the legal ramifications of the Despecialized Edition, Harmáček—echoing Shone's observations about fans who returned repeatedly to the theater to see the Prequels despite not liking the films—argued that his work in no way jeopardizes Lucasfilm's bottom-line since fans like himself have "already bought *Star Wars* 10 times over on DVD" out of brand loyalty, and will continue to do so until a good quality theatrical version of the Original Trilogy is eventually released.[47]

It should also be noted however that in a decidedly ironic twist other *Star Wars* fans, unhappy with the Prequel Trilogy but believing that a set of good movies exist in them somewhere, have revised these films in a manner reminiscent of Lucas's own revising of the Original Trilogy. One version, known as "The Phantom Edit," was created in the early 2000s by out-of-work film editor Mike J. Nichols, whose Burbank apartment was described by the *Los Angeles Times* as "the most notorious rebel outpost . . . this side of the ice planet Hoth."[48] Nichols trimmed a total of eighteen minutes from 1999's *Star Wars Episode I: The Phantom Menace* and a whopping half-hour from 2002's *Star Wars Episode II: Attack of the Clones*. A different fan-editor, going by JeremyMWest-Esquire, has created what he calls an "anti-cheese" edit of *Star Wars Episode III: Revenge of the Sith*, saying that he removed about fifteen minutes from the film.[49] Even more surprising, some fans have even decided to follow the example set by Lucas and engaged in the process of creating their own revised editions of the Original Trilogy; for example, a version of *Return of the Jedi* free of any Ewoks,[50] or one of *A New Hope* in which Chewbacca is also presented with a medal for heroism by Leia at the ceremony on Yavin IV.[51] And while the methods and guiding philosophies of these various groups of fans may differ, all parties agreed on one thing: no one much cared for George Lucas anymore.[52]

47. Eveleth, "The *Star Wars*."

48. Fausset, "A Phantom Menace?" Based on personal communication with Nichols, it should be noted that he disputes the validity of many of the quotes attributed to him in this article, as well as specific details reported by Fausset about his life and work.

49. Liptak, "Include These."

50. Baxter, "Awesome."

51. Wille, "Fan edits."

52. For a list of some other notable fan-edits of the *Star Wars* series see Barry, "Star Wars."

DVD cover for *The Phantom Edit*, a fan-edit of *Star Wars Episode I: The Phantom Menace* by Mike J. Nichols.

In a 2011 review of the *Star Wars* films' Blu-ray debut—for which Lucas once again made *more* alterations not only to the Original Trilogy but to the Prequel Trilogy as well—writer Casey Broadwater went so far as to liken Lucas to former North Korean dictator Kim Jong-il, writing that Lucas's insistence on constantly altering *Star Wars* was an indication that he "has too much power. He can toy around with his creation as much as he'd like, and there's no one to tell him, 'No, George, stop. You're only making it worse.'"[53] Broadwater's remarks, published a year before Lucas's announcement that he would be selling off the *Star Wars* franchise to Disney, not only demonstrates how far the once beloved director had fallen in the eyes of his fans—who now saw him as an artistic tyrant, drunk with power, whose decisions no one could call into question or successfully oppose no matter how bad they may be—but also speaks directly to Lincoln's point about the

53. Broadwater, "*Star Wars.*"

need for a system of checks and balances between the hierophant/story-teller and their congregation.

Such a system serves as a reminder that creators only get to keep telling their stories—and in today's commercial society profiting greatly from them as well—because of their fans. Failure to understand this complex relationship that exists between creators and fans means running the risk of alienating one's congregation of devoted consumers, thereby destroying the myth cycle one has worked so hard to engineer.

This is exactly what happened with Lucas who, in a sarcasm-laden November 2015 interview with *Vanity Fair*, explained that his decision to sell the *Star Wars* franchise to Disney was motivated largely by the fact that he had been subject to a barrage of criticism by fans: "You go to make a movie and all you do is get criticized. People try to make decisions for you about what you're going to do before you do it, and it's not much fun. You can't experiment. You can't do anything. You have to do it a certain way. I don't like that, I never have. I started out as an experimental filmmaker and I want to go back to making experimental films. But of course no one wants to see experimental films."[54]

Analysis and Conclusion

Lucas's complaint that "no one wants to see experimental films" is reflected in certain respects by cultural critic Hiroki Azuma's argument that, in the postmodern era, fans primarily approach movies as a series of recurring—and therefore familiar—visual motifs, "such as characters and settings, or aspects of the design, or the artwork in a key frame." These motifs can be catalogued across the medium as a whole, and their recurrence and recognition form the main source of pleasure.[55] Azuma calls this fixation with the elements of a work the "database theory" of media consumption and argues, in an almost behaviorist mode, that fans are drawn to products which possess such elements while shunning those which deviate from them.[56] Azuma's contentions echo other remarks made by Lucas in a now infamous

54. Robinson, "George Lucas." Readers are strongly encouraged to watch this interview to see Lucas in a particularly raw state. The moment when the interviewer tells him that she loved his debut film *THX 1138* (1971) and he snaps back "Well, no one else did" is notable and extremely telling.

55. Azuma, *Otaku*, 42–44.

56. Ibid., 172.

December 2015 interview with Charlie Rose, during which he criticized the shortsightedness of his fans, who he claimed only want to see the same spaceships fly by again and again.[57] Of course, seeing the same spaceships fly by again and again was exactly what Disney and director J. J. Abrams gave fans in *The Force Awakens*, which brings us back to our original inquiry: Why was the decision to make *The Force Awakens* an almost exact copy of 1977's *Star Wars* the right move? Why was it so successful?

In addition to the insights provided by Azuma, I am reminded of Andrew Britton's description of the "highly ritualized" screening he attended of the 1981 horror movie *Hell Night*. Britton writes:

> It became obvious at a very early stage that every spectator knew exactly what the film was going to do at every point, even down to the order in which it would dispose of its various characters. . . . The film's total predictability did not create boredom or disappointment. On the contrary, the predictability was clearly the main source of pleasure, and the only occasion for disappointment would have been a modulation of the formula, not the repetition of it. . . . Everyone could guess what would happen, and it did happen. In the course of the evening, art had shrunk to its first cause, and I had the incongruous sense, on coming out, of having been invited to participate in communion.[58]

While Britton was notorious for blasting genre films like *Hell Night*—and *Star Wars* for that matter—as being artistically poor, he nevertheless documents their power in bringing people together and openly compares the event to a Christian Eucharist service. Britton furthermore notes that what allows genre films to function in this way is their highly structured and predictable nature, a trait he astutely observes they share with that of religious rituals. In either case those in the audience, be they Christians attending Easter mass or a cavalcade of genre movie fans showing up for an advance screening, are not there to be taken by surprise. Rather they are there to participate in an event with which they are intimately familiar and whose familiarity is a source of comfort for them. It is this ritualized familiarity that Abrams promised *Star Wars* fans coming to see *The Force Awakens* and that Disney aggressively marketed to them, even going as far as to use as

57. This is also the same interview in which Lucas derogatorily referred to Disney as a band of "white slavers," a remark for which he later apologized (Trendacosta, "A Not-So-Brief History").

58. Britton, "Blissing Out," 98–99.

many practical special effects as possible in the film in lieu of more conventional computer generated effects.[59]

In early 2016 at the Tribeca Film Festival, Abrams addressed the criticism he had received from critics like Edelstein regarding the similarities between *The Force Awakens* and the original *Star Wars* saying:

> [*The Force Awakens*] was a bridge and a kind of reminder; the audience needed to be reminded what *Star Wars* is, but it needed to be established with something familiar . . . The weird thing about that movie is that it had been so long since the last one. Obviously the prequels had existed in between and we wanted to, sort of, reclaim the story. So we very consciously tried to borrow familiar beats so the rest of the movie could hang on something that we knew was *Star Wars*.[60]

Here Abrams's acknowledges that in repurposing elements from the original *Star Wars* his aim was to "remind the audience . . . what '*Star Wars*' is" by reestablishing familiar elements while also, in the spirit of a religious reformer, to "reclaim the story" with the clear implication being that he wished to reclaim it for the fans from the apostate Lucas. Abrams's remarks even suggest an Original Trilogy Exclusivist mentality with regard to the films since he claims that his film, *The Force Awakens*, was the first *Star Wars* movie to come out in a long time, a point he clarifies by bringing up and then dismissing the Prequel Trilogy. Clearly when Abrams says, "it had been so long since the last one," he doesn't mean since 2005 when *Episode III: Revenge of the Sith* was released, but rather since *Episode VI: Return of the Jedi* came out in 1983.[61]

However if fans are so hung up on making sure that the canon of *Star Wars* remains unaltered from what was previously established in the theatrical versions of the Original Trilogy, this of course begs the question as to why they would even bother going to see new *Star Wars* films at all when they could simply just rewatch the Original Trilogy over and over again.[62]

59. McKnight, "The Extreme Lengths."

60. Anderton, "J. J. Abrams."

61. Though *The Force Awakens* does contain numerous references to Lucas' Prequel Trilogy, it is also a matter of public record that Abrams personally oversaw the removal of certain Prequel related Easter Eggs in the film such as the presence of podracer banners above Maz Kanata's tavern on Takodana; see Hiatt, "'Star Wars' Strikes Back." For a list of Prequel references that did make it into the *The Force Awakens* see Young, "10 Times."

62. This is the exact scenario outlined by Steven Rubio in his essay "Not the Movie: *King Kong '76*" regarding another notoriously conservative group of film fans, those of

But as theologian Ben Brazil in his review of *The Force Awakens* writes, the "repetition of iconic moments (the father-son confrontation), its reshuffling of character roles (Rey as Luke, Han and Luke borrowing from Obi-Wan), and its re-use of plot structures (or in this case the whole plot) [of the original *Star Wars*] does not necessarily reveal an utter lack of creativity" on the part of the film's makers or, I would argue, a lack of desire among the franchise's many fans for anything new or different. Rather, Brazil writes, such conservatism only "reflects the balance of structure and change embedded in *Star Wars*' intellectual DNA" and the importance of myths adhering to some degree to a certain preset pattern. The downside to this, Brazil notes, is that such steadfast adherence to the sacred canon of a given myth "simply will not support real, boundary-pushing art."[63]

Apparent confirmation of this assessment has come in the form of the multiple filmmakers who have been removed from their role as directors of Disney's new *Star Wars* movies since the release of *The Force Awakens*. Rumors of such disturbances in the Force began in the early summer of 2016 when news leaked that Disney was ordering up to 40 percent of their first prequel, *Rogue One: A Star Wars Story* directed by Gareth Edwards, to be reshot under the supervision of Editor John Gilroy.[64] The following summer brought the announcement that successful comedy film duo Phil Lord and Christopher Miller had been let go from directing a Han Solo spinoff film with the pair citing "creative differences" with the House of Mouse.[65] Only a few months later Disney announced that director Colin Trevorrow would also no longer be helming *Star Wars Episode IX* after coming to "the conclusion that our visions for the project differ."[66]

News of Trevorrow's departure created the biggest shockwaves as the breakout indie director had been responsible for the second highest grossing film of 2015, *Jurassic World*, right behind *The Force Awakens*. As journalist Chris Lee observed in his coverage of the story, the fact that a "bona fide blockbuster filmmaker" like Trevorrow could be so casually dismissed sent

---

the original 1933 *King Kong*.

63. Brazil, "On Nostalgia."

64. For an overview of how these reshoots altered *Rogue One* see Leadbeater, "How *Rogue One*." For an interview with Gilroy about the changes he made to the film see Shepherd, "Rogue One and Suicide Squad." Interestingly, in the later interview Gilroy openly compares *Rogue One* director Edwards' filmmaking style to Lucas', which is probably not the best compliment given the circumstances.

65. Mumford, "Star Wars: Han Solo."

66. Crucchiola, "Colin Trevorrow."

a signal that going forward "no director will ever be bigger than the [*Star Wars*] franchise."[67] Or as Trevorrow himself put it in a subsequent interview, Hollywood is returning "to a time when studios essentially had all of the control and directors were employees."[68] Not surprisingly, in the weeks following the news of Trevorrow's firing Disney announced that the tried-and-true J.J. Abrams would be returning to direct Episode IX.[69]

Whether or not Disney's conservatism with the *Star Wars* franchise will pay off in the end remains to be seen, but as of now the studio has announced their intention to transform *Star Wars* into what they are calling a "Forever-Franchise," with plans to release at least one new *Star Wars* movie every year for as long as audiences keep coming to see them.[70] So far a strict adherence to the narrative formula established by the Original Trilogy appears to have pleased the vast majority of *Star Wars* devotees, who continue to turn out in record numbers for each new installment.[71] At the same time leading critics such as David Ehrlich have described films like *Rogue One* as "a spirited but agonizingly safe attempt to expand cinema's most holy blockbuster franchise"[72]; an apt description which may come to characterize the *Star Wars* series for the rest of its cinematic tenure.

67. Lee, "Colin Trevorrow's Firing."

68. Tabany, "Jurassic World." In the same interview Trevorrow goes on to say that the motivation for this change in the dynamics between movie studios and directors is that studios have become massive corporations and the films they produce are products that need to deliver similarly massive returns at the box office. As a result studios can no longer risk a director following an artistic vision that may not be profitable. Editor John Gilory makes almost the exact same statement in his interview with Jack Shepherd when asked why he was called in to reshoot parts of *Rogue One*.

69. Fleming, "JJ Abrams."

70. Rogers, "The Force."

71. At the time of this writing (January, 2018) the most recent film, 2017's *The Last Jedi* directed by Rian Johnson, is still relatively new, making thoughtful reflection upon it difficult. Nevertheless it should be noted that on Rotten Tomatoes the movie currently has the lowest audience approval rating (49 percent as of January 8, 2018) of any live-action theatrical film in the entire *Star Wars* series—a fact which, true to franchise form, did not stop it from becoming a box office hit and the third highest grossing film of its year. A good deal of the apparent fan backlash appears to stem from the perceived character assassination of Luke Skywalker, who for much of the film is portrayed as a bitter recluse who has lost his faith in the Jedi religion. If true, this would certainly seem to support the contention that *Star Wars* fans tend to reject any dramatic change to the series' mythos—even character development—preferring instead for things to remain mostly static.

72. Ehrlich, "Rogue One."

Bibliography

Alexander, Leigh. "'Gamers' Don't Have to Be Your Audience. 'Gamers' Are Over." *Gamesutra*, October 28, 2014. http://www.gamasutra.com/view/news/224400/ Gamers_dont_have_to_be_your_audience_Gamers_are_over.php.

Anderton, Ethan. "VOTD: 'The Force Awakens' and 'Star Wars: A New Hope' Side-by-Side Comparison Is What You Expect." *SlashFilm*, March 26, 2016. http://www.slashfilm.com/the-force-awakens-and-a-new-hope-comparison.

———. "J. J. Abrams Explains Why 'Star Wars: The Force Awakens' Borrows So Much from 'A New Hope.'" *SlashFilm*, April 16, 2016. http://www.slashfilm.com/the-force-awakens-and-a-new-hope-similarities.

Azuma, Hiroki. *Otaku: Japan's Database Animals*. Translated by Jonathan E. Abel and Shion Kono, Minneapolis: University Of Minnesota Press, 2009.

Barry, Nathan. "Star Wars—The Fandom Editors." *Wired*, February 12, 2013. https://www.wired.com/2013/02/star-wars-fandom-editors/

Baxter, Joseph. "Awesome Star Wars Video Edits the Ewoks out of Return of the Jedi." *Cinema Blend*, 2015. http://www.cinemablend.com/new/Awesome-Star-Wars-Video -Edits-Ewoks-Out-Return-Jedi-70408.html.

Bingley, Matthew. "Copy of Original Star Wars Script Discovered in UNB Library." *CBC News*, June 8, 2015. http://www.cbc.ca/news/canada/new-brunswick/copy-of-original-star-wars-script-discovered-in-unb-library-1.3104206.

Block, Alex Ben. "5 Questions with George Lucas." *The Hollywood Reporter*, February 9, 2012. http://www.hollywoodreporter.com/heat-vision/georgelucas-star-wars-inter view-288523.

Brazil, Ben. "On Nostalgia, Myth, and Star Wars: The Force Awakens." *Sacred Matters*, January 6, 2016. http://sacredmattersmagazine.com/on-nostalgia-myth-and-star-wars-the-force-awakens.

Britton, Andrew. "Blissing Out." In *Britton on Film: The Complete Film Criticism of Andrew Britton*, edited by Barry Keith Grant, 97–154. Detroit: Wayne State University Press, 2008.

Broadwater, Casey. "Star Wars: the Complete Saga Blu-ray Review: Is the Force Strong with This One?" *Blu-ray.com*, September 12, 2011. http://www.blu-ray.com/movies/ Star-Wars-The-Complete-Saga-Blu-ray/14903/#Review.

Cavallaro, Dani. *The Art of Studio Gainax: Experimentation, Style and Innovation at the Leading Edge of Anime*. Jefferson, NC: McFarland, 2009.

Crucchiola, Jordan. "Colin Trevorrow Will No Longer Direct *Star Wars: Episode IX*." *Vulture*. September 5, 2017. http://www.vulture.com/2017/09/colin-trevorrow-will-no-longer-direct-star-wars-episode-ix.html.

Dery, Mark. "Kraken Rising: How the Cephalopod Became Our Zeitgeist Mascot." *H+ Magazine*, May 24, 2010. http://hplusmagazine.com/2010/05/24/kraken-rising-how-cephalopod-became-our-zeitgeist-mascot.

Edelstein, David. "*The Force Awakens* Succeeds by Following the Original *Star Wars* Blueprints." *Vulture*, December 16, 2015. http://www.vulture.com/2015/12/review-star-wars-the-force-awakens.html.

Ehrlich, David. "'Rogue One' Review: The First 'Star Wars' Spinoff Is a Scrappy Space Adventure That Plays Things Painfully Safe." *Indie Wire*, May 26, 2017. http://www.indiewire.com/2016/12/rogue-one-review-star-wars-1201757457.

Eveleth, Rose. "The *Star Wars* George Lucas Doesn't Want You to See." *The Atlantic*, August 27, 2014. http://www.theatlantic.com/technology/archive/2014/08/the-star-wars-george-lucas-doesnt-want-you-to-see/379184.

Fausset, Richard. "A Phantom Menace?" *Los Angeles Times*, June 1, 2002. http://articles.latimes.com/2002/jun/01/entertainment/et-fausset1.

Fleming, Mike, Jr. "JJ Abrams Returning To Director's Chair On 'Star Wars: Episode IX.'" *Deadline Hollywood*. September 12, 2017. http://deadline.com/2017/09/jj-abrams-star-wars-episode-9-director-colin-trevorrow-lucasfilm-disney-1202167681.

"George Lucas Knows You're Arguing About Han Shooting First." *WBUR*, October 6, 2014. http://www.wbur.org/onpoint/2014/10/06/han-shot-first.

Gilsdorf, Ethan. *Fantasy Freaks and Gaming Geeks: An Epic Quest for Reality Among Role Players, Online Gamers, and Other Dwellers of Imaginary Realms*. Guilford, CT: Lyons, 2009.

"Got GOUT? The 2006 Original Version DVD Bonus Feature Fiasco." *Saving Star Wars*, 2010. http://savestarwars.com/gout.html.

HanDuet. "Harmy's Star Wars: Despecialized Edition—History & Sources Documentary (extended version)." YouTube video, 19:58. Posted January 8, 2017. https://youtu.be/mGrXO2RDzLg.

Hiatt, Brian. "'Star Wars' Strikes Back: Behind the Scenes of the Biggest Movie of the Year." *Rolling Stone*. December 2, 2015. https://www.rollingstone.com/movies/features/star-wars-strikes-back-behind-the-scenes-of-the-biggest-movie-of-the-year-20151202.

Hosie, Ewen. "'Star Wars: Despecialized Edition' Restores the Original, Unedited Trilogy." *Vice*, November 17, 2015. https://motherboard.vice.com/en_us/article/jpgxj8/star-wars-despecialized-edition-removes-alterations-to-the-original-trilogy

Jenkins, Henry. *Textual Poachers: Television Fans and Participatory Culture*. 2d edition. New York: Routledge, 2012.

Jůn, Dominik. "The Czech Guerilla Restorationist Battling to 'Save Star Wars.'" *Radio Prague*, August 11, 2014. http://www.radio.cz/en/section/special/the-czech-guerilla-restorationist-battling-to-save-star-wars.

Kijima, Yoshimasa. "The Fighting Game Otaku Community: What Are They 'Fighting' About?" In *Fandom Unbound: Otaku Culture in a Connected World*, edited by Mizuko Ito et al., 249–74. New Haven, CT: Yale University Press, 2012.

Kluthe, Andy and Andrew Bridgman. "The 8 Types of Star Wars Fans." *Dorkly*. February 28, 2014. http://www.dorkly.com/post/59766/the-8-types-of-star-wars-fans.

Leadbeater, Alex. "How *Rogue One: A Star Wars Story* Changed During Reshoots." *ScreenRant*. December 16, 2016. https://screenrant.com/star-wars-rogue-one-reshoots-changes.

Lee, Chris. "Colin Trevorrow's Firing from *Star Wars* Is Another Reminder That No Director Will Ever Be Bigger Than the Franchise." *Vulture*. September 8, 2017. http://www.vulture.com/2017/09/star-wars-episode-8-colin-trevorrow-firing-explanation.html.

Lincoln, Bruce. "Mythic Narrative and Cultural Diversity in American Society." In *Myth and Method*, edited by Laurie L. Patton and Wendy Doniger, 163–76. Charlottesville, VA: University Press of Virginia, 1996.

Liptak, Andrew. "Include These Anti-Cheese *Star Wars* Prequels While You Prepare for *The Force Awakens*." *io9*, December 13, 2015. http://io9.gizmodo.com/include-these-anti-cheese-star-wars-prequels-while-you-1747781701.

"Lucas Talks as 'Star Wars' Trilogy Returns." *Today*, September 15, 2004. http://www.today.com/popculture/lucas-talks-star-wars-trilogy-returns-wbna6011380.

Lussier, Germain. "George Lucas Speaks Out Against Altering Films in 1988." *SlashFilm*, August 31, 2011. http://www.slashfilm.com/george-lucas-speaks-altering-films-1988/

Lyden, John C. "Whose Film Is It, Anyway? Canonicity and Authority in *Star Wars* Fandom." *Journal of the American Academy of Religion* 80:3 (2012) 775–86.

McKnight, Brent. "The Extreme Lengths JJ Abrams Went to Connect The Force Awakens to the Original Star Wars Trilogy." *CinemaBlend*, July 14, 2015. http://www.cinemablend.com/new/Extreme-Lengths-JJ-Abrams-Went-Connect-Force-Awakens-Original-Star-Wars-Trilogy-72581.html.

Mullis, Justin. "Playing Games with the Great Old Ones: Ritual, Play, and Joking within the Cthulhu Mythos Fandom." *The Journal of the Fantastic in the Arts* 26:3 (2015) 512–30.

Mumford, Gwilym. "Star Wars: Han Solo spin-off directors fired after 'creative differences'" *The Guardian*. June 21, 2017. https://www.theguardian.com/film/2017/jun/21/star-wars-han-solo-spin-off-directors-fired-after-creative-differences.

Nelson, Victoria. *Gothicka: Vampire Heroes, Human Gods, and the New Supernatural*. Cambridge, MA: Harvard University Press, 2013.

Price, Robert M. Foreword to "Horror Show" by Gary Myers. In *The Tsathoggua Cycle: Terror Tales of the Toad God*, edited by Robert M. Price, 166. Oakland, CA: Chaosium, 2005.

"Q & A with Van Ling, Rick McCallum, Richard Dean, Pablo Helman, Jon Shenk and George Lucas." September 11, 2001. https://www.thedigitalbits.com/site_archive/articles/starwars1dvd/qanda.html.

Robinson, Joanna. "George Lucas Explains Why He's Done Directing *Star Wars* Movies." *Vanity Fair*, November 18, 2015. http://www.vanityfair.com/hollywood/2015/11/george-lucas-star-wars-jar-jar-binks.

Rogers, Adam. "The Force Will Be With Us. Always." *Wired*, December 21, 2015. https://www.wired.com/2015/11/building-the-star-wars-universe.

Rubio, Steven. "Not the Movie: *King Kong '76*." In *King Kong is Back! An Unauthorized Look at One Humongous Ape*, edited by David Brin with Leah Wilson, 27–35. Dallas: Benbella, 2005.

Saitō, Tamaki. *Beautiful Fighting Girl*. Translated by J. Keith Vincent and Dawn Lawson. Minneapolis: University of Minnesota Press, 2011.

Saler, Michael. *As If: Modern Enchantment and the Literary Prehistory of Virtual Reality*. Oxford: Oxford University Press, 2012.

Scalzi, John. *The Rough Guide to Sci-Fi Movies*. London: Rough Guides, 2005.

Seligman, Adam B., et al. *Ritual and its Consequences: An Essay on the Limits of Sincerity*. New York: Oxford University Press, 2008.

Shepherd, Jack. "Rouge One and Suicide Squad editor talks reshoots, deleted scenes and Star Wars spin-off expectations." *Independent*. January 10, 2017. http://www.independent.co.uk/arts-entertainment/films/features/rogue-one-reshoots-star-wars-spin-off-editor-suicide-squad-john-gilroy-cgi-tarkin-trailer-a-new-hope-a7519996.html.

Shone, Tom. *Blockbuster: How Hollywood Learned to Stop Worrying and Love the Summer*. New York: Free, 2004.

Siede, Caroline. "If You like *Return of the Jedi* but Hate the Ewoks, You Understand Feminist Criticism." *A.V. Club*, September 14, 2015. http://www.avclub.com/article/ if-you-return-jedi-hate-ewoks-you-understand-femin-224765.

Smith, Grady. "'Star Wars: Episode I—The Phantom Menace': Just How Successful Has the 3-D Re-release Been?'" *Entertainment Weekly*, February 21, 2012. http://ew.com/ article/2012/02/21/star-wars-phantom-menace-rerelease-3d-box-office.

Smith, Jonathan Z. "The Bare Facts of Ritual." In *Imagining Religion: From Babylon to Jonestown*, 53–65. Chicago: University of Chicago Press, 1982.

Sullivan, Kevin P. "Star Wars: The Force Awakens, A New Hope Similarities." *Entertainment Weekly*, September 19, 2015. http://ew.com/article/2015/12/19/star-wars-force-awakens-new-hope-similarities.

Tabany, Sebas. "Jurassic World: Fallen Kingdom—Colin Trevorrow." YouTube video, 5:21. Posted December 26, 2017. https://youtu.be/n9xJjPjeDK4.

"This September: Original Unaltered Trilogy on DVD." *Star Wars.com*, May 3, 2006. http://web.archive.org/web/20060615205322/http://www.starwars.com/episode-iv/ release/video/news20060503.html.

Trendacosta, Katharine. "A Not-So-Brief History of George Lucas Talking Shit about Disney's *Star Wars*." *io9*, December 31, 2015. http://io9.gizmodo.com/a-not-so-brief-history-of-george-lucas-talking-shit-abo-1750464055.

Vineyard, Jennifer. "George Lucas Says Indiana's Next Crack of the Whip Will Be Tamer." *MTV*, May 11, 2006. https://web-beta.archive.org/web/20111001112036/http:// www.mtv.com/news/articles/1531527/lucas-next-indiana-jones-will-be-tamer. jhtml.

Wille, Joshua. "Fan edits and the legacy of *The Phantom Edit*." *Transformative Works and Cultures* 17 (2014). http://journal.transformativeworks.org/index.php/twc/article/ view/575/466.

Young, Bryan. "10 Times 'The Force Awakens' Nods to the 'Star Wars' Prequels." *howstuffworks*. December 29, 2015. https://entertainment.howstuffworks.com/10-times-the-force-awakens-nods-the-star-wars-prequels.htm.

CHAPTER 8

MEMORY, HISTORY, AND FORGETTING IN *STAR WARS* FANDOM

SYED ADNAN HUSSAIN

Abstract: A compelling point of intersection between religious studies and fan studies may be found in the exploration of imagination and memory. Scholars such as Danièle Hervieu-Léger have delved into ways in which a discontinuity or splintering of tradition may be seen as a problem of collective memory. Similarly, de-canonization efforts by Disney to reset and rebrand the *Star Wars* universe may be construed as an attempt to restructure the relationship between fans and official content producers. Disney may be attempting to reduce fans, through a process of official forgetting, to mere consumers. Resisting these official shifts may prove to be a test for the resilience of *Star Wars* fans, or at the very least will highlight ways that *Star Wars* fandom must be viewed as multiple traditions.

I first saw *Star Wars* as a bootleg from a rental store, Future Video, near Sheikh Hamdan Street in Abu Dhabi, in the days before the U.A.E. was cool. The print was lousy, the film overexposed and the sound was from before the Ben Burtt '85 mix, but I loved it because it was about a boy from a desert going on to fly spaceships. I watched the beginning and the end more than the middle bits, which felt boring at the time. It would take years for me to see the full trilogy in a clean print, as most of the home versions people had were either in NTSC for the American expats, or Betamax for the Brits—neither was available to our PAL-VHS home. We moved to the United States in the early nineties and I would attend my first fan convention shortly after. In 1993, I hitched a ride from a local comic shop to a trilogy marathon at a nearby convention with a bonus midnight showing of *Dünyayi Kurtaran Adam* ("Turkish Star Wars" 1982).[1] This would be my first encounter with North American *Star Wars* fandom.

A poster for "Turkish Star Wars."

1. *Dünyayi Kurtaran Adam* is a Turkish sci-fi film that borrows unlicensed footage from *Star Wars* as well as newsreel clips to splice together a wonderfully bizarre story that is simultaneously familiar through its takings of recognizable material, and alien through its campy Turkish melodramatic plot. The uninitiated may find copies available on the Internet, but this author recommends that it be watched in company.

These nostalgic communities flocked to small gaming conventions in New England in the 1990s and convened to teach and exchange texts as well as to engage in ritualized viewings and reenactments of the films. These conventions also included communal acts of remembering; in particular, sharing first encounters of the films and role-playing in the Expanded Universe. The rich mythology, informed as it was by Joseph Campbell's theories, felt familiar and almost real and formed the basis for the collective memories of these communities. As such, I wholeheartedly agree with John Lyden's recent statement that, "if there is any popular culture phenomenon that can be referred to as 'religion,' it would be the fandom associated with the *Star Wars* films."[2] He convincingly argues that an expanded understanding of what properly constitutes religion is important for reevaluating our academic categories, and, I would add, for challenging a lingering classism in our field that dismisses fandom as somehow unworthy of study.

The purchase of Lucasfilm by Disney in 2012 was a bombshell for those of us concerned with the future of *Star Wars*. The famously micro-managed franchise was leaving the hands of its creator, and original copyright holder, for one of the most powerful corporate studios in the world. The sale was for an outrageous sum of four billion dollars—more than a dollar from over half the planet. Social media lit up with fans' concerns, intermingled with their excitement, about increased filmic content in the *Star Wars* universe. The universe would, however, need to shrink before it could explode. Two years after the purchase, a decision was made by executives to de-canonize everything in the extended *Star Wars* universe. The jetsam consists primarily of books, comics, and games previously authorized by George Lucas. The new canon includes the new Disney releases as well as

---

2. Lyden, "Whose Film," 775. Sociologists have attempted a few definitions of religion which explicitly deal with *Star Wars* as a religion, including Adam Possamai's "hyper-real religion" (*Religion and Popular Culture*), and Markus Altena Davidsen's "fiction-based religion" ("From Star Wars to Jediism"). Possamai defines hyper-real religion as "a simulacrum of a religion created out of, or in symbiosis with, commodified popular culture which provides inspiration at a metaphorical level and/or is a source of beliefs for everyday life" ("Yoda Goes to Glastonbury," 20). For Davidsen, who himself draws on Steve Bruce, religion "assumes the existence of transempirical realities" such as supernatural entities or "principles of moral purpose (e.g., karma, ma'at)." Jediiism, based on *Star Wars*, is therefore a religion because it satisfies these needs (Davidsen, "From Star Wars to Jediism," 377). The condition of modernity that allows for both these definitions is an increasing individuality and domination of market mentalities that essentially sees modern subjects as "shopping" for meaning in a marketplace of ideas (Carrette and King, *Selling Spirituality*).

the original six films and the *Clone Wars* TV series.[3] The statement posted on the official *Star Wars* website is cold, unsigned, and states plainly that the de-canonization was implemented "in order to give maximum creative freedom to the filmmakers and also preserve an element of surprise and discovery for the audience." Anything previously written is not being discarded "but presented under the new Legends banner."[4]

The collective memory of a community depends on stability and continuity to the past. For *Star Wars* fan communities, the collapse of the Expanded Universe fundamentally shifts the ways in which they relate to *Star Wars*. The stories and characters they may have loved, named children after, or argued over were erased from the new official memory of *Star Wars*, and their own experience was relegated to some other universe. As an academic fan, or Aca-Fan to use Henry Jenkins's term, I am interested in exploring the ways that this act constitutes a break in the chain of memory that undergirds *Star Wars* fandom as a *tradition*. The theory of fans that I will rely on draws from the first generation of fan studies, which takes inspiration from the author/reader binary in the literary theories of Barthes and Foucault. The crisis created by the sale and the shift in authority may be seen as a problem of individual memory and collective memory and a challenge to those communities that order themselves around a connection to past traditions. To that end, I apply the theories of sociologist Danièle Hervieu-Léger, who explicitly connects memory and continuity with community and tradition, as a way of seeing the crisis of canonicity as a challenge to the cohesion of a "religious group." We may come to appreciate de-canonization as an attempt to restructure fan communities or to erase them. Milan Kundera, quoting Milan Hübl, would put it thusly: "[t]he first step in liquidating a people . . . is to erase its memory. Destroy its books, its culture, its history. Then have somebody write new books, manufacture a new culture, invent a new history. Before long the nation

3. This change was effected in part through the collapsing of the multi-tiered canon system which consisted of G-canon or George canon including Lucas's prerogative to change the universe through films and other media; T-canon or television canon; C-canon or continuity canon, which includes a majority of the Expanded Universe; S-canon or secondary canon such as the Holiday Special; N-canon or non-canon such as "what if" stories (Whitbrook, "A Brief History").

4. To add insult to injury, the banner image for the article is of Timothy Zahn's *Heir to the Empire* but with its new de-canonized "Legends" cover ("The Legendary Star Wars").

will begin to forget what it is and what it was. The world around it will forget even faster."[5] The extraordinary plot similarities between *The Force Awakens* (2016) and *A New Hope* (1977) may even compel the analysis of the recent film as a soft-reboot of the universe. To accept Kylo Ren, fans have to kill Jaina and Jacen Solo.[6]

Jaina and Jacen Solo action figures (produced by Hasbro).
Photo courtesy of Denis Achilles del Callar.

An example of an absence of collective memory would be the alienation felt by immigrants or refugees in strange lands. In my own experience, when I first came to the United States as a teenager I had no connection to the collective memory of the United States, barring Alex Haley's *Roots*, which was in constant circulation on Pakistani television. Its narratives, its

5. Kundera, *The Book of Laughter and Forgetting*, 159.

6. In the bestselling *Thrawn* trilogy Han Solo and Leia Organa have twins Jaina and Jacen Solo, a family that was erased in *The Force Awakens* to make room for Kylo.

history and its politics were, as they would label me, alien. Lewis A. Coser reflects on a similar immigrant alienation in his introduction to Maurice Halbwachs' watershed book *On Collective Memory.*[7] Coser claims that as an immigrant he felt an "impassable barrier" between himself and "native Americans" as a result of his not "sharing enough collective memories."[8] Individual memory and remembering is not enough for societal cohesion; for that you need a socialized cultural memory. Benedict Anderson pulls together similar ideas in his exploration of the way that the "fiction" of the nation state is created through acts of remembering and forgetting in his brilliant *Imagined Communities.*

In *Religion as a Chain of Memory,* Hervieu-Léger draws upon Halbwachs to cultivate a definition of religion that pivots on collective memory. Her intention is to overcome the failure of sociology's conceptual tool kit, which imagined religion's inevitable decline and disappearance. For Hervieu-Léger, scholars were simply looking in the wrong places. Rather than focusing on the content of belief, she shifts the task of the scholar to a focus on "*the mutating structures of believing* that these changes in content partially reveal."[9] She defines religion as "an ideological, practical, and symbolic framework that constitutes, maintains, develops, and controls the consciousness (individual or collective) of membership to a particular heritage of belief."[10] Beliefs, for her, are those convictions that "give meaning and coherence to the subjective experience of those that hold them.[11] "Within this perspective," then, "one designates as 'religious' all forms of believing that justify themselves, first and foremost, upon the claim of their inscription in *a heritage of belief.*"[12] This heritage of belief relies on "*a chain of memory,* the continuity of which transcends history."[13] For established traditions, such as Roman Catholicism, the challenge of modernity is an attack on the "continuity of belief" in the face of an "imperative to change."[14]

For Hervieu-Léger, in a society that suffers the collapse of traditional institutions such as the family, individuals may cling to other socializing

7. Halbwachs and Coser, *On Collective Memory.*

8. Ibid., 21.

9. Hervieu-Léger, "Religion as Memory," 253.

10. Ibid., 256.

11. Ibid., 253.

12. Ibid., 256.

13. Ibid., 257 (emphasis in original).

14. Ibid., 257–58.

forces such as "elective fraternities," which in turn may present as religious once they can "incorporate the idea of [their] own continuity beyond the immediate context of its members' interrelating."[15] She gives the extraordinary example of the cult-following of Jim Morrison, which evolved into something religion-like through the establishment of and appeals to distinct lineages of followers.[16] This analysis would be similarly relevant to other "elective fraternities" that may have religious elements, such as *Star Wars* fan communities, most explicitly in the form of Jediism, which has cultivated a creedal (and pastoral) structure based on politically liberal notions such as non-discrimination on the basis of sexual orientation, cultivating compassion, and self-determination.[17] James Cox, in his analysis of Hervieu-Léger's categories, praises her for the way that the definition pivots on the following question: "How is the act of believing legitimized?"[18] If fans believe, in what ways is their belief legitimized? Moreover, are their beliefs to be protected from a corporate takeover and possibly asserted against copyright holders? The question we must ask is who controls the process of legitimization? And what structures are created to preserve these traditions?

On some level, *Star Wars* canonicity has always been troublesome. George Lucas continued to edit the original films until their Blu-ray release in 2011,[19] and has loudly refused to allow the original theatrical version to be archived in the National Film Registry, claiming in 2004: "The special edition, that's the one I want out there. The other movie, it's on VHS, if anybody wants it . . . To me, it doesn't really exist anymore. It's like this is the movie I wanted it to be, and I'm sorry you saw the half a completed film and fell in love with it. But I want it to be the way I want it to be."[20] The strangeness of this variety of auteur, who can effectively edit out of history the creative contributions of other artists involved in the process of production, is unimagined—a god-auteur that can bend time and space and even attempt to rescript memory. Some fans, in response, have seen themselves as "Rebels" fighting to protect *Star Wars* from its creator. These include websites such as SaveStarWars.com and OriginalTrilogy.com and a

15. Hervieu-Léger, *Religion as a Chain of Memory*, 152.

16. Hervieu-Léger, *Religion as a Chain of Memory*, 152.

17. Temple of the Jedi Order, "Doctrine."

18. Cox, "Religious Memory," 9.

19. Chitwood, "More Changes."

20. Associated Press, "Lucas Talks."

Despecialized Edition project led by Petr "Harmy" Harmáček, which many fans, myself included, consider the definitive digital version of the original 1977 film.[21] These fans refused to be bullied into forgetting their connection to the 1977 release. In a somber, if not bitter, interview with Charlie Rose in 2015, Lucas admits that he is unhappy about his legacy, claiming, "I finally realized that, no matter what happens, I'm never going to get out. I'm always going to be George 'Star Wars' Lucas, no matter how hard I try to be something else."[22] In the same interview, Lucas later admits that in surrendering *Star Wars* he sold his "kids" to "white slavers."[23] I wonder if, in retrospect, fans will miss the antagonism of their relationship with George Lucas—anger is not indifference. Disney, however, has the option to remain indifferent to fan criticism by appealing to a broader consumer desire for more content. Some fans have begun to fire back, and have accused Disney of trying to influence opinion about the prequels before the launch of *The Force Awakens* with a series of paid-for-content articles to improve the brand's marketability.[24]

In his typology of forgetting, as it is related to cultural memories, Paul Connerton explores seven distinct kinds of forgetting. Lucas's actions may fit into the category of "repressive erasure," and the forgetting being required by Disney as they retract and expand the universe suggests "planned obsolescence."[25] The differentiation in kinds of forgetting will help us expose the power structures between fans and the owners of copyright. For Connerton, a repressive erasure is an attempt by the powerful, the state for example, to force a forgetting that both denies "historical rupture" while simultaneously creating a "historical break." A classic historic example would be the Roman practice of *damnatio memoriae*, wherein

21. HanDuet, "Ultimate Introductory Guide."

22. Lucas, Interview.

23. Lucas, Interview.

24. RedLetterMedia, "Mr. Plinkett's."

25. Connerton, "Seven Types of Forgetting." The seven types are: 1) Repressive erasure: e.g., totalitarian revision of history; 2) Prescriptive forgetting: public acknowledgment and decision to forget to move forward; 3) Forgetting that is constitutive in the formation of a new identity: e.g., a new relationship requires "forgetting" previous ones; 4) Structural amnesia: remembering that which is relevant or tied to prestige; 5) Forgetting as annulment: this refers to the process of "discarding" from a surfeit of information; 6) Forgetting as planned obsolescence: this is the core of capitalist and consumerist forgetting—the new model of computer requires new software, new licenses; 7) Forgetting as humiliated silence: Connerton gives the example of Germany after the end of the war in which the population had to rebuild a devastated country.

a traitor or enemy of the state would be official erased from history by destroying statutes, confiscating land, and removing their names from official records.[26] Lucas's claim that the previous versions of the original trilogy no longer exist, and his desire to ensure that they will not be allowed to exist, exposes a power play. His decision is total, and his refusal to submit the original films to the national archive is an attempt both at repression and erasure; the original versions die by fiat. Disney's purchase of the *Star Wars* universe expunges the auteur's vision and replaces it with the metrics of the market. Take for example the *Spider-Man* franchise, which is on its third reboot despite every iteration being financially successful. This kind of planned obsolescence for Connerton is "an essential ingredient in the operation of the market" as it is the process by which we discard to create space for the new.[27] The sheer number of films planned—ten before 2020—will inevitably expand the universe in ways never anticipated by the first generations of *Star Wars* fans.

Arguably, after the initial consumerist frenzy that marked "*Star Wars* mania" between 1977 to 1983, the period of relative quiet that followed allowed the slow expansion of the universe through a licensing program. Fans were aware of plot inconsistencies between series, and there was a general policy of only allowing cameos of major characters until Timothy Zahn's bestselling *Thrawn* trilogy, which relaunched excitement in *Star Wars* communities in the 1990s by continuing the story, with official sanction, where the movies left off. But perhaps just as importantly, between 1982 and 1993 the home video versions, through the new medium of VHS and Betamax, made possible the endless rewatchings that would be an important hallmark of this phase of *Star Wars* fandom. These technologies had made what Roland Barthes would refer to as "rereading" possible.

Roland Barthes, in "La mort de l'autheur" (a pun on Malory's *Le Morte d'Arthur*), states that "the birth of the reader must be at the cost of the death of the Author."[28] His essay was an assault on traditional literary criticism, which Barthes claimed was obsessed with exploring the author's identity in a search for the true meaning of a text or a single "'theological' meaning (the 'message' of the Author-God)."[29] He was contrasting this view with the idea of a text as a "multi-dimensional space in which a

26. Connerton, "Seven Types of Forgetting," 60.

27. Ibid., 57.

28. Barthes, "The Death of the Author," 148.

29. Ibid., 146.

variety of writing, none of them original blend and clash . . . [It] is a tissue of quotations drawn from the innumerable centres of culture."[30] Barthes's goal was to set the text free from its author, and give the text to its readers with their myriad engagements. Barthes would inspire Henry Jenkins, a pioneer of fan studies, who used the idea of "rereading" to understand the ways in which fans develop a creative relationship to "texts" by reinterpreting and appropriating or "poaching."[31] Barthes conceives of rereading as "an operation contrary to the commercial and ideological habits of our society, which would have us 'throw away' the story once it has been consumed ('devoured'), so that we can move on to another story, buy another book."[32] It is through the practice of rereading that readers resist being reduced to mere consumers. Jenkins would add that fans participate in multiple modes of discursive engagement, and even if they were behaving as consumers that it was a form of critical consumption.[33] This is well illustrated in the film *The People vs. George Lucas*, which explores fan hostility towards the Special Editions and the Prequels. These readers were desperate for the "death" of the author (Lucas).

Foucault is similarly interested in authors and authorship but, typical of his analytics, he is similarly unconcerned by whom the real author may be, and instead asks "What are the modes of existence of this discourse? Where does it come from; how is it circulated; who controls it?"[34] I revisited Foucault for this essay not merely because he offers his work up readily as "tool boxes . . . to short circuit, discredit or smash systems of power," but also because his philosophy emerges from the ashes of the Second World War and the restructuring of the European public sphere, which had to survive trauma through extraordinary acts of memory, memorializing, and forgetting.[35] The intellectual as a participant in the public culture may be obliged to look to the margins and the marginalized, not to represent those that cannot represent themselves (the Saidian sin), but rather to contribute our knowledges and techniques to the struggle against domination, erasure, and forgetting. In Foucault's language, this approach is that of the Nietzschean "genealogy." Foucault understands genealogy to be a coupling

30. Barthes, "The Death of the Author," 146.
31. Jenkins, *Textual Poachers*.
32. Barthes, *S/Z*, 15–16.
33. Jenkins, *Textual Poachers*.
34. Foucault, "What Is an Author," 138.
35. Foucault, *Power, Truth, Strategy*, 115.

of "scholarly erudition" and "local memories" to deploy knowledge of past struggles for use in "contemporary tactics."[36] Jonathan Arac brilliantly describes this genealogical practice as one that "transforms history from a judgment on the past in the name of present truth to a 'counter-memory' that combats our current modes of truth and justice, helping us to understand and change the present by placing it in new relation to the past."[37] Counter-memory was Foucault's response to the idea of a stable collective or cultural memory that was in service of power, the kind of cultural memory deployed as weapon by fascists and Nazis.

The fundamental schism created by de-canonization and revision in the *Star Wars* universe should be conceived as a crisis of collective memory or as a break in the chain of a tradition. This does not mean that a tradition ceases to exist, but rather it transforms or splinters into separate traditions that will construct their relationship to an authoritative past differently. By way of example, take the infamous "Han shot first" incident. In the original theatrical release, Han Solo engages in banter with a bounty hunter whom he then shoots dead using a concealed weapon. In the 1997 Special Edition, Lucas (in the most ham-handed re-edit in film history) has Greedo the bounty hunter shoot first and miss, hitting the wall with a drawn and aimed weapon at point blank range, after which Han shoots him down. I felt a deep unease as I watched Han Solo's self-sacrifice in *The Force Awakens* as his act must be read completely differently by fans who believe that he did or did not shoot first. A "scoundrel" who was willing to kill a bounty hunter in cold blood may seek redemption through heroic self-sacrifice. But if Han refuses to murder and only draws second, he fits a very different trope of the noble self-sacrificing hero. Having two profoundly different arcs for the same central character is a point of schism.

It may be critical to identify, as Hervieu-Léger suggests, the ways in which individual *Star Wars* communities structure themselves as lineages that both accept or reject the official collective memory being aggressively asserted by the new rules of canon. It may be that it simply does not make sense to speak of *Star Wars* fans as a community with a single collective memory but rather as ones that define themselves on a distinct structuring of canon and tradition that may reject, co-opt, or poach the official authorized canon. If there is an official collective memory of *Star Wars*, then there is also a counter-memory that refuses to see the tradition as

36. Foucault, *Society Must Be Defended*, 8.
37. Arac, *Postmodernism*, xviii.

something that can be sold or erased and that is deeply suspicious of the ways in which the universe will expand *ad nauseum*. The din of endless new content interferes with the core anti-consumerist practice of rereading that Jenkins (by way of Barthes) saw as critical to fan communities. One of the dangers of the corporatization of *Star Wars* is that it may risk reducing fans, especially new fans, to mere consumers, or will channel their creativity into authorized forms such as the official *Star Wars* website or the endlessly expanding Comic Cons that have increasingly become advertising venues for the next year's commercial and filmic products.

Star Wars fandom in particular has been marked historically by a love/hate relationship with George Lucas that came to a head in his attempts to assert sole ownership of what many fans had guarded and grown in his absence. The sale, however, is far more troubling in the ways that it ultimately expects fans to be consumers if they wish to continue seeing installments in a beloved franchise. Disney ultimately benefits from any fan engagements with their brand, as long as the brand itself and potential market expansion are protected. Moreover, if we further our analysis of *Star Wars* fandom as religion, then does copyright infringement operate as a state-sanctioned heresy charge that protects the orthodox position? Take for example the recent lawsuits against Michael Brown, who operates a "Lightsaber Academy," alleging trademark infringement and unfair competition (yes, seriously), after Lucasfilm denied him a licence to operate.[38] Disney's statement is that they must protect their intellectual property from profiteers, and on the surface that seems to make sense—but if Michael Brown understands himself to be a Jedi, represents himself as such on a census, and is simply trying to teach his tradition of belief, is it an over-entanglement of government and religion to use copyright to limit his free exercise? The structures of power as enforced through law and copyright are inherently biased against fans that make a religion of content with commercially held licenses. J.R. Carrette and Richard King offer us some wisdom on this point: "If capitalism is indeed the new triumphant ideology of our times and Marxism its apparently defeated heresy, what we need at this moment in history are new 'atheisms' that reject the God of money."[39] The practice of these new atheisms may include rereading and rejecting the *Star Wars* brand and its official consumerist logic, and celebrating acts of rebellion such as stealing or streaming.

38. McCann, "Classes."

39. Carrette and King, *Selling Spirituality*, 179.

Ultimately *Star Wars* was a smart buy. *The Force Awakens* made back over half of the four billion dollars paid for the franchise. What remains to be seen is if the films will continue to be as derivative as Episode VII or if they will break new ground. I am skeptical about the future of the franchise as it promises to drown the central fan rereadings in endless pastiche. Disney has realized that adding *Star Wars* to a title is an instant guarantee of commercial success and we shall undoubtedly begin to see genre films that are in essence *Star Wars* horror, or *Star Wars* buddy comedies. But fans will not sit still for bland recapitulations; they will continue to choose what to affirm and what to deny. And as scholars study the evolution of *Star Wars* fandom, they must recognize that there is no single tradition but instead multiple traditions, each of which negotiates its relationship to the Disney franchise in unique ways. Although Emperor Lucas may hate this, a thousand flowers are blooming in the fan creativity that resists, invents, restores, and renews their own visions of what *Star Wars* has meant to them.

Bibliography

Anderson, Benedict R. *Imagined Communities: Reflections on the Origin and Spread of Nationalism*. London: Verso, [1983] 2006.

Arac, Jonathan. *Postmodernism and Politics*. Minneapolis: University of Minnesota Press, 1986.

Associated Press. "Lucas Talks as 'Star Wars' Trilogy Returns." *Today*, September 15, 2004. http://www.today.com/popculture/lucas-talks-star-wars-trilogy-returns-wbna6011380.

Barthes, Roland. "The Death of the Author." In *Image, Music, Text*, edited and translated by Stephen Heath, 142–48. New York: Hill and Wang, 1977.

———. *S/Z*. Translated by Richard Miller. New York: Hill and Wang, 1974.

Carrette, J. R., and Richard King. *Selling Spirituality: The Silent Takeover of Religion*. London: Routledge, 2005.

Chitwood, Adam. "More Changes to STAR WARS Include Blinking Ewoks and Different Cut of Greedo Shooting First." September 1, 2011. http://collider.com/star-wars-blu-ray-changes-2.

Connerton, Paul. "Seven Types of Forgetting." *Memory Studies* 1:1 (2008) 59–71.

Cox, James. "Religious Memory as a Conveyor of Authoritative Tradition: The Necessary and Essential Component in a Definition of Religion." *Journal of the Irish Society for the Academic Study of Religions* 2 (2015) 5–23.

Davidsen, Markus. A. "From *Star Wars* to Jediism: The Emergence of Fiction-based Religion." In *Words: Religious Language Matters*, edited by Ernest van den Hemel and Asja Szafraniec, 376–89. New York: Fordham University Press, 2014.

Foucault, Michel. *Power, Truth, Strategy*. Edited by Meaghan Morris and Paul Patton. Sydney: Feral, 1979.

————. *Society Must Be Defended: Lectures at the Collège de France, 1975-76.* Edited by Mauro Bertani and Alessandro Fontana. Translated by David Macey. New York: Picador, 2003.

————. "What Is an Author?" In *Language, Counter-memory, Practice: Selected Essays and Interviews,* edited by Donald F. Bouchard, translated by Donald F. Bouchard and Sherry Simon, 113–38. Ithaca, NY: Cornell University Press, 1977.

Halbwachs, Maurice, and Lewis A. Coser. *On Collective Memory.* Chicago: University of Chicago Press, 1992.

HanDuet. "The Ultimate Introductory Guide to Harmy's Star Wars Trilogy Despecialized Editions v4.8.1." January 2, 2017. https://docs.google.com/document/d/1yLsvexWB VM8IYSGopKuSfsGk5YIgCwQWd23bqb5ryD4/pub.

Hervieu-Léger, Danièle. "Religion as Memory: Reference to Tradition and Constitution of a Heritage of Belief in Modern Societies." In *Religion: Beyond a Concept,* edited by Hent de Vries, 245–58. New York: Fordham University Press, 2008.

————. *Religion as a Chain of Memory.* New Brunswick, NJ: Rutgers University Press, 2000.

Jenkins, Henry. *Textual Poachers: Television Fans and Participatory Culture.* New York: Routledge, 1992.

Kundera, Milan. *The Book of Laughter and Forgetting.* New York: Knopf, 1980.

"The Legendary Star Wars Expanded Universe Turns a New Page." *Starwars.com,* April 25, 2014. http://www.starwars.com/news/the-legendary-star-wars-expanded-universe-turns-a-new-page.

Lucas, George. Interview with Charlie Rose. *Charlie Rose,* December 25, 2015. https://charlierose.com/videos/23471.

Lyden, John. C. "Whose Film Is It, Anyway? Canonicity and Authority in *Star Wars* Fandom." *Journal of the American Academy of Religion* 80:3 (2012) 755–86.

McCann, Erin. "Classes for Jedis Run Afoul of the Lucasfilm Empire." *New York Times,* October 19, 2016. https://www.nytimes.com/2016/10/20/business/media/lucasfilm-sues-jedi-classes.html.

Possamai, Adam. *Religion and Popular Culture: A Hyper-Real Testament.* New York: Peter Lang, 2005.

————. "Yoda Goes to Glastonbury: An Introduction to Hyper-real Religions." In *Handbook of Hyper-real Religions,* edited by Adam Possamai, 1–21. Leiden: Brill, 2012.

RedLetterMedia. "Mr. Plinkett's The Star Wars Awakens Review." YouTube video, 1:45:07. Posted October 2, 2016. https://youtu.be/miVRaoR_8xQ.

Temple Of The Jedi Order. "Doctrine of the Order." *Temple Of The Jedi Order: International Church of Jediism.* February 12, 2007. https://www.templeofthejediorder.org/doctrine-of-the-order.

Whitbrook, James. "A Brief History of Star Wars Canon, Old and New." *io9.* February 2, 2015. http://io9.gizmodo.com/a-brief-history-of-star-wars-canon-old-and-new-1683320381.

Zahn, Timothy. *Heir to the Empire.* New York: Bantam, 1991.

————. *Dark Force Rising.* New York: Bantam, 1992.

————. *The Last Command.* New York: Bantam, 1993.

CHAPTER 9

THE ION **CANON** WILL FIRE SEVERAL SHOTS TO MAKE SURE ANY ENEMY SHIPS WILL BE OUT OF YOUR FLIGHT PATH

Canonization, Tribal Theologians, and Imaginary World Building[1]

KENNETH MACKENDRICK

Abstract: This essay draws on Jonathan Z. Smith's redescription of canon and religious authority in order to better understand canon and *Star Wars* fandom and franchise. Disney's announcement relegating the *Star Wars* Expanded Universe to the non-canonical Legends banner is discussed, followed by fan responses to this announcement. In light of an analysis of the stratification of transmedial narrative into canonical and non-canonical spheres, it is apparent that franchise and fandom can be redescribed in terms of canonization and authority, wherein canonization refers to the creation and authorization of a shared imaginary world.

Canon and Authority

Jonathan Z. Smith's essay "Sacred Persistence" sets out to redescribe a characteristic category of religious experience and expression: canon

1. A special thanks is due to the students of RLGN 2222 The Supernatural in Popular Culture. Their responsiveness to the topic and course readings made this essay possible. Additional thanks must also be extended to Ken Derry: encore!

147

and its authority.[2] The redescription is important given the traditional emphasis on the varied canonical content and not on the strategies employed by authorities creating, maintaining, and interpreting the canon. According to Smith, a canon is a subtype of the genre list. A list is characterized by its discontinuity and its more or less arbitrary inclusions and exclusions. If lists exhibit clearly ordered principles of organization we can speak of catalogs. Catalogs are heterogeneous but possess codes of classification for the purpose of information retrieval. Catalogs are subject to principles of organization imposed by the interpretive interests of an exegete but may contain implicit norms generated by the assumed features of the itemized list.[3] The principled nature of catalogical organization also allows content to be extended to include contingent novelties.[4]

For Smith, a catalog is transformed into canon by means of interpretive closure. Closure occurs when the list is held to be complete. Closure is only possible in the presence of an authorized interpreter. Smith writes:

> Where there is canon, it is possible to predict the *necessary* occurrence of a hermeneute, of an interpreter whose task it is continually to extend the domain of the closed canon over everything that is known or everything that exists *without* altering the canon in the process. It is with the canon and its hermeneute that we encounter the necessary obsession with exegetical totalization.[5]

Smith proposes divination as a prototypical example. The requirements for items on a canonical list are fairly minimal: the items in question must be able to bear an obsessive interpretive load.[6] Shifting emphasis away from the haphazard content of the canon to strategies manipulating the canon is a move in the right direction. Rather than focus on the intrinsic qualities of itemization, interpretive authorization is the key to understanding canonization.

---

2. Smith, *Imagining Religion*, 36.

3. On the mechanics of generation, see Walton, *Mimesis as Make-Believe*, 138–87.

4. Smith, *Imagining Religion*, 44–45.

5. Ibid., 48.

6. The interpretive obsession with totalization, the applicability of the canon to all aspects of life, is a hallmark characteristic of practices often deemed religious. Smith cites Cicero and Freud in this regard. Briefly, Smith sees religious activity as a concern with little details that, by means of displacement, are turned into matters of great and urgent importance (Smith, *Imagining Religion*, 38–39).

I start with Smith in the hope of establishing a bit of reciprocity between the comparative history of religion and the study of popular
culture. The more we think about canonization in *Star Wars*, the more
we can learn about canonization in the context of beliefs and practices
commonly deemed religious (with an emphasis here on the ordinariness
of "religion").[7] Similarly, bringing insights from the comparative history
of religion to popular culture should help us understand popular culture
better (or, at least, differently).[8]

Smith's redescription of canon in the context of the comparative history of religion can be usefully aligned with Mark J. P. Wolf's discussion
of canonicity. Wolf understands canon as the idea that "certain things are
'true' for an imaginary world."[9] In contrast to Smith's exemplar of divination, Wolf focuses on circles of authorship, the overlapping weave of contributions in the creation of an imaginary world, from "the originator and
main author to estates, heirs, and torchbearers; employees and freelancers;
the makers of approved, derivative, and ancillary products that are based
on a world; and finally to the noncanonical additions of elaborationists and
fan productions."[10] The difference between Smith's conception of canon and
Wolf's is mainly a matter of emphasis, although there is one striking distinction. Smith argues that canon must be understood in the context of an
authorized interpreter and sets out a program of study to examine strategies
of canon creation and canonical manipulation. Wolf's account is more of a
genealogy of how imaginary worlds are built. I see their respective studies
as complementary, especially in the context of canonicity and franchise, but
if we follow Smith's lead it is important to recognize the instrumental role
played by canonizing authorities.

If we relate Smith's redescription of canon and authority to the *Star
Wars* franchise, and do so with Wolf's emphasis on circles of authorship
(or, authorization) and world-building, our focus turns not to the imaginary world represented by canonical materials but to the activities and

7. Bloch, "Why Religion"; McCutcheon, "Redescribing Religion."

8. "Studying the way that popular culture fandom mirrors religious practice may
illuminate the changing nature of religion as much as it illuminates the practices of popular culture" (Lyden, "Whose Film," 783). For an instructive analysis of failures of parity
and reciprocity in comparative studies, see Smith, *Drudgery Divine*, 36–53. Michael
Saler's otherwise excellent study of imaginary world building is marred, in my view, by
its conscious exclusion of religion as exemplary of this process (Saler, *As If*, 3–23).

9. Wolf, *Building Imaginary Worlds*, 270.

10. Ibid., 269.

strategies of authors and authorities managing the canon. Our emphasis is drawn away from the content of the *Star War* universe to the contours of canonization, the strategies used by authorities to interpret, construct, or deconstruct application and relevance.

With regard to *Star Wars*, it is important to recognize the role of franchise in canon creation and interpretation. As defined by Henry Jenkins, franchising is "the coordinated effort to brand and market fictional content within the context of media conglomeration."[11] Canonization is always in play when it comes to transmedial narratives and franchises (movies, books, comics, video games, radio plays, toys, fan fictions, and so on).[12] The degree to which the canon is open is primarily, although not exclusively, governed by the franchise, usually centralized in the hands of intellectual property right holders.[13] This makes a franchise the primary curator of the canon and their interpretations and productions tend to have a high degree of normative authority. That being said, it is worth keeping in mind that a franchise is an ongoing business and its products may be seen as little more than a series of trademarks and properties to be protected. Stockholders may have little overt interest in creating an epic universe.[14] *Star Wars* is exemplary because Lucasfilm's emphasis on canon was fairly well defined and often a matter of public discussion.[15] It is also helpful to keep in mind that interpretive authorities may not be originators or authors of the canon. For example, while George Lucas is the originator of *Star Wars* and Timothy Zahn is an author of numerous novels set in the *Star Wars* universe, their

11. Jenkins, *Convergence Culture*, 326.

12. In Smith's essay, canon is defined as a closed list. Myth, however, is defined as open (*Imagining Religion*, 48). Bringing canon and myth (and myth-making) together is instructive, especially under the rubric of social formation. For a brief overview of myth and myth-making, see McCutcheon, "Myth." For overviews of social formation, see Redden, "Social Formation" and Brown, "Mythmaking and Social Formation." On myth as ideology in narrative form, see Lincoln, *Theorizing Myth* and *Discourse and the Construction of Society*.

13. I would add that opening, closing, and rebooting the canon constitutes a crucial activity of franchise management.

14. Brooker, *Using the Force*, xvi.

15. As Wolf reports, the *Star Wars* Holocron (the franchise's database) is organized into five levels of canonicity: G-canon (films, scripts, novelizations, Lucas's statements), T-canon (television shows, e.g., *Star Wars: Clone Wars*), C-canon (Expanded Universe elements), S-canon (material from *Star Wars* role-playing games), and N-canon (non-canonical material). Wolf, *Building Imaginary Worlds*, 271.

input on canon may or may not carry interpretive authority with fans, other authors, or intellectual property right holders.[16]

The artificiality of the convention of copyright, of assigning interpretive authority to property right holders, should not be underestimated (nor, I suppose, should the sanctions for dissent!).[17] Although it might seem natural to assume that canonical power is intrinsic to copyright, this is clearly not the case. Copyright is a strategy of authorization, one particular way of manipulating canonical categories. Not every franchise succeeds in controlling the scope and range of its brand. According to Teemu Taira, Jediism likely attracts interest with little or no regard for who owns the franchise or the image presented by the franchise owners. On the contrary, as a "discourse on religion" Jediism has been taken up as a vehicle for expressing social protest.[18] It is easy to imagine members of Jediism to be largely indifferent to corporate ownership and interpretation. In other words, Jediism may be viewed best not as a subculture of *Star Wars* fandom but as a niche strategy for particular kinds of political or social protest. Even copyright holders have to compete for legitimacy.

As mentioned, one of the tenets of Smith's redescription of canon is closure: a catalog is drawn into canon by means of completion.[19] In the case of *Star Wars*, however, the canon is open. The *Star Wars* franchise forms a complicated and permeable entity with multiple openings and porous boundaries. For competing interpreters, this is a bit of a problem. How do you maintain interpretive authority in a franchise? Certainly ownership of property rights and trademarks carry a significant authoritative load. The power to sanction competing interpreters and interpretations is not an insignificant power. Smith refers to competing authorities as "tribal theologians," rival exegetes engaged in efforts to further manipulate the canon. Historically, *Star Wars* fans have had a role in the maintenance and rejection of proposed canonical categories and, to some degree, an influence over content as well. Consumption and creative expression shape the catalog and the canon.[20]

16. Especially after the release of *Episode I: The Phantom Menace*. See Brooker, *Using the Force*, 79–99.

17. For a relevant discussion, see Tushnet, "Legal Fictions."

18. Taira, "The Category of 'Invented Religion.'" See also the discussions by Porter, "I am a Jedi," and McCormick, "The Sanctification of *Star Wars*."

19. Smith, *Imagining Religion*, 48.

20. The inclusion of the 501st Legion (a fan-based organization) into the *Star Wars* canon is one of several examples that could be cited. See Taylor, *How Star Wars Conquered*

Given these complexities, in the context of franchise it makes sense to speak of canonization instead of canon. Canonization describes a much more diverse spectrum of activities and strategies than we see in Smith's preliminary account of authority and canon. Circles of authorship, contestations about canon, and varying levels of interpretive authorization are part of the canonization process. Smith is aware of this dynamic: "in some complex situations, there may be a further need to develop parallel, secondary traditions that will recover the essentially open character of the list or catalog."[21] Citing Henry Maine, Smith adopts the term "legal fiction" to describe processes and strategies of canonical alteration. Applied to *Star Wars*, this insight suggests that it is a mistake to get involved in the so-called "Canon Wars" (debates about continuity and canon with reference to the *Star Wars* universe).[22] As Smith reminds us, the continuity prized by canonizers and fans is not to be had at the level of the list or catalog. There is no resolution to debates about canon; tribal theologians compete for authority to interpret, merchandise, and parody aspects of the imaginary world of *Star Wars*. Lists and catalogs are by definition discontinuous, which is why exegetes should be the primary figures in any study of canonization.[23] Invested parties compete to apply the canon to various aspects of life in accord with their interests.

As an open-ended process, canonization is a contested public sphere of imagination. As discussed by Michael Saler, a public sphere of imagination is a place where fans and interested parties gather and transform imaginary worlds into virtual worlds: "public spheres of the imagination enabled their participants to relate the virtual world to the real world in a critical manner, turning fantasy into a social practice."[24] As Smith observes,

---

the Universe, 31. The tension between Lucasfilm and Slash fiction is an example of a more confrontational relation (Brooker, *Using the Force*, 129–71). For a good discussion of the relation between fandom and industry see Jenkins, *Convergence Culture*, 135–73.

21. Smith, *Imagining Religion*, 50.

22. For a sample of these debates, see Brooker, *Using the Force*, 101–13. In Brooker's discussion one fan (Jedi Knight Seyrah) bristles through the pretenses of canon: "Canonism is an illusion . . . it's all a story . . . Lucas can contradict himself if he likes" (113). Wolf plausibly distinguishes between stories and world-building. If we adopt the "it's all a story" perspective we must simultaneously abandon the imaginary world of the *Star Wars* universe (Wolf, *Building Imaginary Worlds*, 198–225).

23. This is why so much of the work on *Star Wars* as myth is tedious. Once myth is defined, *Star Wars* is studied on the basis of its analogous content. It seems to me that such analyses assume the very thing in question: what counts as *Star Wars*? Who decides?

24. Saler, *As If*, 94.

application is not a generalized process but "a homiletic endeavor, a quite specific attempt to make the 'text' speak to a quite particular situation."[25] This application may have to do with marketing and the creation of new world-building works but may also function like a pep rally to uplift the fans and generate solidarity or franchise buzz. Application of canon (what I'm tempted to refer to as myth-making) is always in the service of a wide range of social formations and social interests.

Taking the work of Smith and Wolf one step further, I would like to speculate about the effects of canonization; not simply in relation to authority, but with regard to shared imaginary worlds: what does canon do, what does this authorization accomplish?

Canon Wars: An Awakening

On October 2012 the Disney corporate umbrella purchased Lucasfilm for a reported $4.05 billion. While many were delighted to welcome Leia into the sisterhood of Disney princesses, there was also a good deal of ambivalence about the new owners of the *Star Wars* franchise, the incoming interpretive authority. Most fans responded to Disney's acquisition of Lucasfilm with cautious optimism. A few expressed dismay, a small minority horror and disgust. On the whole it seems fans were excited. Not since *Episode 1: The Phantom Menace* and its siblings had fans experienced this kind of titillation.[26]

After the merger, but before *Episode VII: The Force Awakens* appeared, William Proctor studied fan reactions. The ambivalence reported by fans, as Proctor explains, mainly concerned questions about the canon and continuity of the *Star Wars* universe. As is well known, *Star Wars* fans have a particular fascination with continuity and the pleasures of the serial[27]—so much so that an interest in continuity and consistency must be understood to be one of the central preoccupations and defining characteristics of fan culture in general.[28] For those inclined towards the *Star Wars* Expanded Universe, this feeling of cautious optimism was also a premonition of the cataclysmic rupture of the *Star Wars* canon in 2014.

25. Smith, *Imagining Religion*, 51.

26. Proctor, "Holy Crap," 198.

27. For overviews, see the entries "*Star Wars* Canon" in *Wikipedia* and "Canon" in *Wookiepedia*.

28. Duncan et al., "Continuity" (cited in Proctor, "Holy Crap," 219).

On 25 April 2014 Disney made an announcement that relegated the canonical *Star Wars* Expanded Universe to legend. Kathleen Kennedy, Lucasfilm President, explained that a new master "story group" would oversee and manage the *Star Wars* universe. She also declared:

> In order to give maximum creative freedom to the filmmakers and also preserve an element of surprise and discovery for the audience, *Star Wars* Episodes VII-IX will not tell the same story told in the post-*Return of the Jedi* Expanded Universe. While the universe that readers knew is changing, it is not being discarded . . . Demand for past tales of the Expanded Universe will keep them in print, presented under the new Legends banner.[29]

Del Ray publisher's Editor at Large Shelly Shapiro further commented,

> Legends are things that are often told over generations . . . they change constantly with the telling, so you can't actually attribute an author to any particular one. Often it wasn't someone who was actually there. You can go back to any of the legends . . . they're pretty sure there was a 'King Arthur,' but most of the stories probably did not happen. But that doesn't mean there aren't kernels of truth in it . . . Everything now—starting from "A New Dawn" on—is canon. So if you care about that—which you really probably shouldn't, but if you do—it's all a part of this whole new collaborative process . . . All of this stuff happened. But not really; it's fiction.[30]

Without having to scroll too far into the comments in this and related posts we find the following:

> Hoykraut: THIS IS OUTRAGEOUS, (I know I'm about 1 standard galactic year out of touch on this). What happens to all the millions of pages of media that have been put out there in the last 30 years? Am I simply supposed to forget all of the material I have read and played and watched for the last 20 something years of my life? The EU is practically a part of my soul![31]

> Visitor421: What a load of bull. I won't accept wiping the slate clean. I will not have anything to do with this scam. I have about 80 books on my shelf, tens of games and hours of emotion, laugh and tears. This is like awakening at the age of 40 and people telling me you are memory-flashed clone. I have been horribly robbed. I

29. "The Legendary *Star Wars.*"

30. Shapiro cited in Dyce, "'Star Wars' Creatives."

31. Outlaw, "'Star Wars' Official Canon," #comments.

will not pay to have my memory overwritten/scrambled. You lost a long time customer. I have to admit that in my anger I hope the new timeline will financially crash, burn and never recover. All good comes to an end and the tale has ended. You know where you can shove your canon.[32]

For many indifferent to *Star Wars*, this discussion must appear a bit strange. Why would the president of Lucasfilm make a public announcement about the fictional status of the events depicted in the movies and novels of *Star Wars*? Doesn't this go without saying? And what does it mean to say that some of the *Star Wars* stories are legends with kernels of truth while other stories are true? And what happens when the canonical characters in *Star Wars Rebels* make reference to de-canonized characters and events?

Most commentators immediately and sympathetically observed that many fans were "understandably upset" by the announcement.[33] But why? Why is this understandable? If *Star Wars* is fiction, why be concerned whether some of its stories are truer than others?

Given the paradoxical quality of these statements, we should not fail to see that the stratification of narratives, stories, and catalogs into canonical and non-canonical is an ingenious interpretive move. Few fans question the appropriateness of the category "canon," even when it was suggested by Shapiro that fans shouldn't care about this kind of stuff.[34] Discourses about canon and continuity appear to be non-negotiable characteristics of fandom. While the comment seems designed to buff the ongoing canon wars, there is more to it than that.[35]

As mentioned, canonization is the key to transmedial franchise. The utility of canon for franchise need not be discussed much further here and its role within fandom and the "Canon Wars" can also be put to the side for the moment. What might attract our interest is the way in which

32. Outlaw, "'Star Wars' Official Canon," #comments.

33. Dyce, "'Star Wars' Creatives."

34. This comment has an interesting rhetorical payload: it suggests that fans shouldn't be concerned about canonical continuity even when this interest is one of the defining features of fandom. This playful rhetorical gesture constitutes and reveals part of the attractiveness of canonization: fans at play selectively apply their interest in continuity (Thon, "Converging Worlds," 29). Playful contradictions facilitate interest. See also Luhrmann, "Serious Play."

35. As mentioned, contesting canon and continuity is part and parcel of what fans do. Fans will recognize each other by T-shirts or memes such as: "*Star Wars* is not Episode IV: A New Hope, it's *Star Wars*" or "Han Shot First" or "Why did George Lucas try to ruin *Star Wars* by turning the force into an exact science?"

canonization naturalizes the authority of an interpreter and simultaneously transforms fictional narratives into "shared imaginary worlds."[36]

Canonization and Imaginary Worlds

Canons play an integral role in the interpretive future of a community. As Wolf notes, "for a work to be canonical requires that it be declared as such by someone with the authority to do so."[37] The job of the exegete is to maneuver the relevance of a canon over time: canonization must meet the demands of a comprehensive doctrine. The exegete has a range of strategies at their disposal. For example, a canon can be subject to strategic openings and closures; or an interpreter may subtract items from an existing catalog (*Star Wars Holiday Special*), or add more to the catalog by incorporating novelties—perhaps by rearranging the organizational principles or retconning innovative creations (501st Legion). The interpreter may also pave the way for future authorized (and unauthorized) productions and manipulations. Jan-Noël Thon makes an interesting distinction between canonical and apocryphal worlds in the intersubjective construction of universes (e.g., HBO's *Game of Thrones* versus George Martin's *A Song of Ice and Fire*), perhaps a useful distinction for thinking about the acquisition of Lucasfilm by Disney.[38] These tactical shifts are made possible by the stratifying of fictional works into canonical and non-canonical spheres. It is my contention that canonization is the process that manufactures a shared imaginary world.[39] The "canon" is a strategic deployment, assembling the catalog into a complete unit.[40] Canonization is a strategy of totalization, a

36. An imaginary world is rooted in narrative fiction or in the creation of a paracosm and could be distinguished from an imaginary social world. An imaginary social world consists of our real and fantasized relationships. See Caughey, *Imaginary Social Worlds* as well as Honeycutt, *Imagined Interactions*.

37. Wolf, *Building Imaginary Worlds*, 271.

38. Thon, "Converging Worlds," 37.

39. In this context shared means normative. Each individual will have a distinct mental representation of an imaginary world, but insofar as these representations function to coordinate activities they are normative. For a good discussion, see Thon, "Converging Worlds." Thon's account focuses on the importance of narrative intention. Following Jürgen Habermas, I would add the semantic and action-coordination features of intersubjective communication (Habermas, *The Pragmatics of Communication*).

40. The fictional status of *Star Wars* does not make it an inappropriate candidate for comparison with religion. On the contrary, canonization is a means through which the imagination is leveraged into the realm of shared social facts and norms.

move that creates a boundary around the catalog. It is a world-constituting declaration. Non-canonical works are unworldly, in this sense.

If, as Smith notes, canon demarcates a reduction and the interpretation an overcoming of that reduction, the canon is constituted by the discontinuous stuff used for the creation of a continuous shared imaginary world. Once canonized, the arbitrary assemblage of items takes on a totalizing function. The canon and its authorities establish an imaginary world as a *world* that can be rendered modestly as a fictional world or instantiated more vigorously as a virtual world. The "worldly" character of the "*Star Wars* universe" is an effect of the process of canonization.

It follows that imaginary worlds don't just exist, they have to be maintained and authorized in an actual social context (what Habermas calls a practical discourse). It doesn't make any sense to talk about a dead imaginary world: imaginary worlds are practical and participatory.[41] Imaginary worlds are authorized into existence by means of authoritative interpreters and those who sanction this authorization. Movies, novels, role-playing games, video games, and comics all form a rather messy and discontinuous collection of materials. Also, the transformation of fantasy fiction into a virtual reality by means of canonization should not be confused with delusion. A delusion is when someone comes to accept a fictional world as real (often the result of systematic distortions in perception).[42] What happens with the authorization of imaginary worlds is more akin to the creation of an interstitial realm where the boundary between narrative fiction and social fact is obviated.[43] In this way imaginary worlds are similar to wrestling in Roland Barthes's interpretation. In the most successful fights there is a

41. In contrast to John Searle's emphasis on social ontology, I would argue that imaginary worlds have a deontological status. The shared and contested status of imaginary worlds speaks to our shared understanding of their features and our interest in the relevance of those features to the so-called real world.

42. Hirstein, *Brain Fiction*, 19.

43. On interstitiality, see Arnal and McCutcheon, *The Sacred is the Profane*, 156–62. For good studies of the permeability of the imagination in relation to reality, see Harris, *The Work of the Imagination*; see also his excellent study of the role of testimony in construction our sense of reality in *Trusting What You're Told*. For interesting studies of the blurring boundaries between narrative fiction and "fact," see Lévi-Strauss, "The Sorcerer and His Magic"; Cusack, "Discordianism"; Laycock, "How Role Playing Games Create Meaning"; Baker, *The Zombies are Coming!* Many of these studies are apropos of Evans-Pritchard's observation about the interstitial quality of fieldwork in "Some Reminiscences."

kind of "frenzied fantasia in which laws, rules of the game, the censure of referees, and the limits of the Ring are abolished."[44]

The "worldliness" of the "*Star Wars* universe" is maintained by canon in a double sense: as an imaginary world (an intersubjective construction with normative elements) and as an imaginary world related to the real world. This explains the never-ending debates about canon, continuity, and appropriateness.[45] The declaration of canonical status creates a social fact about the comprehensiveness and applicability of a catalog. An imaginary world is a reservoir of potential applications, which may include everything from political allegory and cultural parody to fan fiction and merchandise. The *Star Wars* universe *is* because it is authorized as a shared imaginary world.

While it may seem that there is no substantial comparison between religious canon and *Star Wars* canon, I would argue that the similarity resides in that canonization obviates the boundary between fact and fiction by means of normative governance and relevance. In this way, the comparison is particularly telling.[46] Perhaps a third comparison with food could be mentioned, again following Smith's lead.

Smith notes that there appears to be "virtually no limits to what people can and do eat if looked at globally." However, there appears to be the most "stringent limits on what any particular group of people can and will eat, and a most intense reluctance to alter these boundaries."[47] What we consider to be food is subject to a remarkable limitation. Cuisine, however, is characterized by variegation. Canon establishes limitation and an interpreter ingeniously overcomes the limitation to produce interest and variety.[48] The point I am adding here is that the interpretation, the overcoming of reduction, participates in world-creation. We have, after all, the "world of French cuisine" and the "world of Chinese cuisine" as well as "the world of raw food." The degree to which these worlds "exist" is matched by the degree to which an authority can be identified, a guarantor of the proper way

---

44. Barthes, *Mythologies*, 12.

45. I'm tempted to suggest that this dynamic also explains fan fascination with the "making of" supplements of imaginary world creation. Documentaries and commentaries assist fans in the "proper" interpretation and understanding of canon, what Kathleen Kennedy refers to as the "rules" of *Star Wars* (Kennedy in *Secrets of* The Force Awakens).

46. I've explored this idea from a slightly different angle in MacKendrick, "We Have an Imaginary Friend in Jesus."

47. Smith, *Imagining Religion*, 39.

48. Ibid., 40.

of understanding something. Imaginary worlds disappear when authorities evaporate into a cultural haze.[49]

Imaginary worlds may also "disappear" by means of sustained criticism. The project of demythologizing the Bible, for example, aims to disaggregate the canonical and imaginary biblical worldview into its unrelated list items. Demythologization has as its project the deconstruction of worlds, showing how the world was produced by little more than an ensemble of arbitrary texts and contexts lorded over by an authority.[50]

The fragility of imaginary worlds is in part a result of a constant need for rejuvenation. Interpretive authorities have to compete for relevance. This is exemplified in the remedial characteristics of *The Force Awakens* and *Rogue One*. Both aim to generate a "feeling of authenticity" (Kennedy) by branching out from material contained in the original trilogy. At the same time, the narrative and style needs to appeal to a new generation. Doug Chiang, Lucasfilm Head of Design, discusses this in terms of going back to the core features that made the original trilogy so great: the concept designs of Ralph McQuarrie (a brilliant interpretive maneuver!). David Gilford, Production Designer, talks about *The Force Awakens* as a period piece.[51] Kathleen Kennedy nicely encapsulates the dilemma of the tribal theologian: "we can go through a period of nostalgia, but what are we going to do with future generations who want to step into their own era of the vast mythology and universe called *Star Wars*?"[52] So, while the creators of next generation of *Star Wars* films are looking to the future, they are also managing the past, engaging in innovative "legal fictions" and manipulating the canon for an incoming set of social interests.

In conclusion, canonization is a process that is predicated upon the assumed authority of an interpreter. Interestingly, canonization also participates in the establishing of "imaginary worlds." Such worlds are established and maintained by means of cooperative participation. Imaginary worlds become virtual worlds when they are shared and related to particular contexts. At the level of application, the distinction between narrative and reality is obviated: the point at which an imaginary world becomes a normative

---

49. It is important to note that canon cannot be attributed to "tradition" or "culture." Canon and canonization are active, living processes. See Bayart, *The Illusion of Culture Identity*, for a critique of "tradition," "culture," and "identity" as stable sources of norms.

50. For a relevant study see Mack, *A Myth of Innocence.*

51. Kennedy, Chiang, and Gilford in *Secrets of* The Force Awakens.

52. Kennedy in *The Stories.*

influence on social action. This fusion of fiction and social fact instantiates a fascinating kind of interstitiality and, hopefully, provides us with some insight into our ability to live very largely in imaginary worlds.[53]

Bibliography

Arnal, William E., and Russell T. McCutcheon. *The Sacred is the Profane: The Political Nature of "Religion."* Oxford: Oxford University Press, 2013.

Baker, Kelly. *The Zombies are Coming! The Realities of the Zombie Apocalypse in American Culture.* New York: Bondfire, 2013.

Barthes, Roland. *Mythologies.* Translated by Richard Howard and Annette Lavers. New York: Hill and Wang, 2013.

Bayart, Jean-François. *The Illusion of Cultural Identity.* Translated by Steven Rendall, et al. Chicago: University of Chicago Press, 2005.

Bloch, Maurice. "Why Religion Is Nothing Special but Is Central." In *In and Out of Each Other's Bodies: Theory of Mind, Evolution, Truth, and the Nature of the Social,* 23–40. Boulder, CO: Paradigm, 2013.

Brooker, Will. *Using the Force: Creativity, Community and Star Wars Fans.* New York: Continuum, 2002.

Brown, Ian Philip. "Mythmaking and Social Formation in the Study of Early Christianity." *Religion Compass* 10:1 (2016) 15–24.

"Canon." *Wookiepedia, the Star Wars Wiki.* http://starwars.wikia.com/wiki/Canon.

Caughey, John L. *Imaginary Social Worlds.* Lincoln, NE: University of Nebraska Press, 1984.

Cusack, Carole M. "Discordianism: Chaos is a Goddess." In *Invented Religions: Imagination, Fiction and Faith,* by Carole M. Cusack, 27–52. Burlington, VT: Ashgate, 2010.

Duncan, Randy, et al. "Continuity." In *The Power of Comics: History, Form, and Culture,* 2nd ed., by Randy Duncan, et al., 319–22. New York: Bloomsbury, 2015.

Dyce, Andrew. "'Star Wars' Creatives Explain Why Canon Vs. Expanded Universe Shouldn't Matter." *ScreenRant.* http://screenrant.com/star-wars-extended-universe-explained.

Evans-Pritchard, E. E. "Some Reminiscences and Reflections on Fieldwork." In *Witchcraft, Oracles, and Magic among the Azande,* by E. E. Evans-Pritchard, 250–54. Oxford: Claredon, 1976.

Habermas, Jürgen. *On the Pragmatics of Communication.* Edited by Maeve Cooke. Cambridge, MA: MIT Press, 1998.

Harris, Paul. L. *Trusting What You're Told: How Children Learn from Others.* Cambridge, MA: Belknap Press, 2012.

———. *The Work of the Imagination.* Oxford: Blackwell, 2000.

Hirstein, William. *Brain Fiction: Self-Deception and the Riddle of Confabulation* Cambridge: MIT Press, 2006.

Honeycutt, James M. *Imagined Interactions: Daydreaming about Communication.* Cresskill, NJ: Hampton, 2003.

---

53. In response to Bloch's provocation in "Why Religion."

Jenkins, Henry. *Convergence Culture: Where Old and New Media Collide.* New York: New York University Press, 2006.

Laycock, Joseph P. "How Role Playing Games Create Meaning." In *Dangerous Games: What the Moral Panic over Role-Playing games Says about Play, Religion, and Imagined Worlds,* by Joseph P. Laycock, 179–209. Oakland, CA: University of California Press, 2015.

"The Legendary *Star Wars* Expanded Universe Turns a New Page." *StarWars.com.* http://www.starwars.com/news/the-legendary-star-wars-expanded-universe-turns-a-new-page.

Lévi-Strauss, Claude. "The Sorcerer and His Magic." In *Structural Anthropology,* by Claude Lévi-Strauss, 167–85. Translated by Claire Jacobson. New York: Basic, 1963.

Lincoln, Bruce. *Discourse and the Construction of Society: Comparative Studies of Myth, Ritual, and Classification, Second Edition.* Oxford: Oxford University Press, 2014.

———. *Theorizing Myth: Narrative, Ideology, and Scholarship.* Chicago: University of Chicago Press, 1999.

Luhrmann, T. M. "Serious Play: The Fantasy of Truth." In *Persuasions of the Witch's Craft: Ritual Magic in Contemporary England,* by T. M. Luhrmann, 324–36. Cambridge, MA: Harvard University Press, 1989.

Lyden, John C. "Whose Film Is It, Anyway? Canonicity and Authority in *Star Wars* Fandom." *Journal of the American Academy of Religion* 80:3 (2012) 775–86.

Mack, Burton. *A Myth of Innocence: Mark and Christian Origins.* Philadelphia: Fortress, 1988.

MacKendrick, Kenneth G. "We Have an Imaginary Friend in Jesus: What Can Imaginary Companions Teach Us about Religion?" *Implicit Religion* 15:1 (2012) 61–79.

McCormick, Debbie. "The Sanctification of *Star Wars*: From Fans to Followers." In *Handbook of Hyper-real Religions,* edited by Adam Possamai, 165–84. Leiden: Brill, 2010.

McCutcheon, Russell T. "Myth." In *Guide to the Study of Religion,* edited by Willi Braun and Russell T. McCutcheon, 190–208. New York: Continuum, 2000.

———. "Part 1: Redescribing Religion as Something Ordinary." In *Critics Not Caretakers: Redescribing the Public Study of Religion,* by Russell T. McCutcheon, 3–39. Albany: State University of New York Press, 2001.

Outlaw, Kofi. "'Star Wars' Official Canon & Expanded Universe Differences Explained." *ScreenRant.* http://screenrant.com/star-wars-story-group-new-canon-vs-expanded-universe.

Porter, Jennifer. "'I Am a Jedi': Star Wars Fandom, Religious Belief, and the 2001 Census." In *Finding the Force of the Star Wars Franchise: Fans, Merchandise, and Critics,* edited by Matthew Wilhelm Kapell and John Shelton Lawrence, 95–114. New York: Peter Lang, 2006.

Proctor, William. "'Holy Crap, More *Star Wars*! More *Star Wars*? What If They're Crap?': Disney, Lucasfilm and Star Wars Online Fandom in the 21st Century." *Participations: Journal of Audience and Reception Studies* 10:1 (2013) 198–224.

Redden, Jason. "Social Formation and the Study of Religion." *Religion Compass* 9:12 (2015) 501–11.

Saler, Michael. *As If: Modern Enchantment and the Literary Prehistory of Virtual Reality.* Oxford: Oxford University Press, 2012.

Secrets of The Force Awakens: *A Cinematic Journey.* Directed by Laurent Bouzereau. 2016. Disc 2. *Star Wars: The Force Awakens.* Blu-Ray. Burbank: Buena Vista Home Entertainment, 2016.

Smith, Jonathan Z. *Drudgery Divine: On the Comparison of Early Christianities and the Religions on Late Antiquity.* Chicago: University of Chicago Press, 1990.

———. *Imagining Religion: From Babylon to Jonestown.* Chicago: University of Chicago Press, 1982.

"*Star Wars* Canon." *Wikipedia.* Accessed April 7, 2017. https://en.wikipedia.org/wiki/Star_Wars_canon.

The Stories: The Making of Rogue One: A Star Wars Story. Directed by Glen Milner and Ian Bucknole. 2017. Disc 2. *Rogue One.* Blu-Ray. Burbank: Buena Vista Home Entertainment, 2017.

Taira, Teemu. "The Category of 'Invented Religion': A New Opportunity for Studying Discourses on 'Religion.'" *Religion and Culture* 14: 4 (2013) 477–93.

Taylor, Chris. *How Star Wars Conquered the Universe: The Past, Present, and Future of a Multibillion Dollar Franchise, Revised and Expanded.* New York: Basic, 2015.

Taylor, Marjorie. "Do Older Children and Adults Create Imaginary Companions?" In *Imaginary Companions and the Children Who Create Them,* 134–55. Oxford: Oxford University Press, 1999.

Thon, Jan-Noël. "Converging Worlds: From Transmedial Storyworlds to Transmedial Universes. *StoryWorlds: A Journal of Narrative Studies* 7:2 (2015) 21–53.

Tushnet, Rebecca. "Legal Fictions: Copyright, Fan Fiction, and a New Common Law." *Loyola of Los Angeles Entertainment Law Review* 17:3 (1997) 651–86.

Walton, Kendall L. *Mimesis as Make-Believe: On the Foundations of the Representational Arts.* Cambridge, MA: Harvard University Press, 1990.

Wolf, Mark J. P. *Building Imaginary Worlds: The Theory and History of Subcreation.* New York: Routledge, 2012.

SUBJECT INDEX

AUTHOR INDEX

FILM AND TELEVISION INDEX

STAR WARS MEDIA INDEX

Made in the USA
Monee, IL
27 August 2020